JOKES MY MOTHER NEVER TOLD ME

D1603139

MARC BARRY

A Shapolsky Book

For any additional information, contact:
Shapolsky Publishers, Inc.
136 West 22nd Street, NY, NY 10011

1 2 3 4 5 6 7 8 9 10

Library of Congress Cataloging-in-Publication Data

Barry, Mark

Jokes My Mother Never Told Me

I.Title

ISBN: 0-944007-30-9

Typesetting by: Woodmill Press, Somerville, NJ

TABLE OF CONTENTS

ACKNOWLEDGMENTS

First of all, I'd like to thank my Mother, Ruth, for never telling me any of these jokes! Then, I'd like to thank my Dad and Brother, Paul and Wayne, for selling this book in their store (even though they don't know it yet!).

Special thanks to my friend, Steven Abrams, my ears on the floor of the stock exchange, and to the Bilello Brothers, the funniest guys on the Comex!

Last, but not least, loving thanks to my wife, Kathleen, who married me for my jokes, and to my son, Joshua Evan, the funniest one-year-old in the world!

APPETEASERS!

Why is Rob Lowe like a black lung?
>⇨*Because they're both found in minors!*

Did you hear about the latest fashion craze in China?
>⇨*Tank-Tops.*

What do they teach tank drivers there?
>⇨*How to park on a slope!*

Why did the Chinese tank break down?
>⇨*There was a chink in the gears!*

Did you hear about the Chinese student who went out for a couple of drinks and wound up getting tanked?

MORE TO COME...

APPETEASERS!

What's the difference between Salman Rushdie and Elvis Presley?

> ⇨ *Rushdie's dead!*

Have you picked up a copy of Rushdie's new book?

> ⇨ *It's called, "Buddha: The Fat Fuck."*

What do Yuppies call oral sex?

> ⇨ *"sixty-something"!*

Why don't Libyans mix driving education with sex education?

> ⇨ *It would wear the shit out of the camels!*

Did you hear about the dyslexic who tried to commit suicide?

> ⇨ *He threw himself behind an oncoming train!*

MORE TO COME...

POLITICS: A QUAYLE IN HAND IS
WORTH TWO BUSHES

What are the five scariest words in America today?
  ⇨ *"Dan, I'm not feeling well."*

What's Dan Quayle's favorite Viet Namese city?
  ⇨ *Toronto!*

Did you hear what Dan's wife, Marilyn, said to him the other night after making love?
  ⇨ *"You're no Jack Kennedy!"*

Did you hear what Minnie Mouse bought Mickey for his birthday?
  ⇨ *A Dan Quayle watch!*

Did you hear about the movie that's coming out that's all about Dan Quayle's war experiences?
  ⇨ *It's called "Full Dinner Jacket!" It's rated `PG,' as in `Picked by George!'*

MORE TO COME...

What baseball team did Dan Quayle play for?

⇨ *The Dodgers!*

What do you get when you cross Dan Quayle with a Greek?

⇨ *A waiter who won't serve!*

What's Dan Quayle's favorite song?

⇨ *"Over here, Over here!"*

What does Dan Quayle have in common with Yoko Ono?

⇨ *They're both yellow and live off inheritances!*

What's the difference between Dan Quayle and Jane Fonda?

⇨ *Jane went to Viet Nam!*

MORE TO COME...

What's the Dan Quayle weight-loss program?

⇨ *Running from the draft!*

How can you tell when Dan Quayle is ready for battle?

⇨ *He's got his jogging suit on!*

Do you know why all the lesbians voted for Dukakis?

⇨ *'Cause they wanted to lick Bush!*

Do you know why President Bush takes his wife with him wherever they go?

⇨ *So he doesn't have to kiss her goodbye!*

Do you know what Dan Rather has in common with panty-hose worn inside out?

⇨ *They both rub Bush the wrong way!*

MORE TO COME...

GIMME SOME HEDDA!

Have you had the Hedda Nussbaum luncheon-plate special yet?

⇨ *You get a club sandwich, black-eyed peas and poundcake!*

Did you hear what Hedda said when she was asked what is Joel's occupation?

⇨ *"Beats the shit out of me!"*

What's Joel Steinberg's favorite song?

⇨ *"First Time Ever I Broke Your Face."*

What's Joel's favorite rock groups?

⇨ *Wham and The Grateful Dead!*

What did Hedda get for Christmas?

⇨ *Her two front teeth!*

MORE TO COME...

AN A-BUNDY-ANCE OF JOKES!

Did you hear who just quit smoking?

⇨ *Ted Bundy!*

Do you know where he ate his last meal?

⇨ *The Sizzler!*

Do you know what he had there?

⇨ *Juice, then toast!*

Do you know what his last occupation was?

⇨ *Conductor!*

Did you hear that he got a great deal on some furniture?

⇨ *Yeah, he bought a sofa and an ottoman, and they gave him the chair!*

MORE TO COME...

SICK SELEBRITIES!

What do you get when you jerk off into a golf bag?

⇨ *Ickey Woods!*

What did Lloyd Bentsen say to Kitty Dukakis?

⇨ *"I've seen you drink Scotch and...you're no Joan Kennedy!"*

What do you call a roomful of empty Scotch bottles?

⇨ *Kitty Litter!*

What's the ultimate one-night stand?

⇨ *A date with Ted Bundy!*

Why is Mrs. Bundy wearing a wide-brimmed hat?

⇨ *Because she just had a sun-burn!*

MORE TO COME...

NASTY KNEE-SLAPPERS!

What did the people of Lockerbie, Scotland get for Christmas?

⇨ *Luggage!*

Why can't you go to the bathroom at Newmark & Lewis?

⇨ *'Cause Dick Lewis is watching!*

How do you know who gives good blowjobs?

⇨ *Word of Mouth!*

What's the best thing to come out of a dick?

⇨ *The wrinkles!*

Why are gas station attendants like wives?

⇨ *Because when they're not around, you have to pump it yourself!*

MORE TO COME...

KNOCK-OUT PUNCHLINES

Who had the most hits in the 1980's?

⇨ *Hedda Nussbaum!*

Did you hear that Mike Tyson is now dating Hedda Nussbaum?

⇨ *He likes a woman who can take a punch!*

What do you call Mike Tyson with no arms and legs?

⇨ *Nigger!*

Why didn't Robin Givens change her name?

⇨ *Because she didn't want people to know she was Robin Tyson! (robbin' Tyson)*

What are the two worst things that Robin Givens can say to a man?

⇨ *"I do," and "I'd like you to meet my mother!"*

MORE TO COME...

RACE-Y RETORTS

Why can't you circumcise an Iranian?

⇨ *Cause there's no end to those pricks!*

What has 10,000 arms, 10,000 legs and stands three feet tall?

⇨ *The Armenian Hilton!*

Did you hear about the new mayor of Armenia?

⇨ *Barney Rubble!*

What does a Black woman get every time she has an abortion?

⇨ *$500 from "Crime-Stoppers."*

What do a lobster, shrimp and a Chinese man run over by a steam-roller have in common?

⇨ *They're all crushed-Asians!*

MORE TO COME...

PERILS IN THE PERSIAN GULF

What was the most tragic thing about the Iranian airliner being shot down?

⇨ *There were three empty seats!*

What was the temperature that day?

⇨ *290 Below!*

Do you know the difference between an F-14 and an A-300 airbus?

⇨ *No? Would you like to work for the government?*

Did you know that after the tragic accident all the 7-11's were flying their flags at half-mast?

⇨ *They were in mourning because they lost 290 trainees!*

What's the difference between an Iranian and a box of shit?

⇨ *The box!*

MORE TO COME...

OLYMPIC MEDDLING!

Why are steroids like hurricanes?

⇨ *They both make Jamaicans run fast!*

What is Ben Johnson doing nowadays?

⇨ *He's the world's fastest janitor!*

What do gold medals have in common with testicles?

⇨ *They both hang below Greg Luganis' chin!*

Did you hear that Luganis was stripped of his medals?

⇨ *They found traces of Carl Lewis in his urine sample!*

What's Bruce Kimball's new motto?

⇨ *"Don't drink and dive!"*

MORE TO COME...

THE CHOKE'S ON YOU!

What's a Robert Chambers cocktail?

⇨ *A hi-ball with a twist!*

Why can't Robert Chambers trade commodities?

⇨ *He doesn't know the difference between a strangle and a straddle!*

Why isn't Robert Chambers good in bed?

⇨ *Because he chokes during sex!*

What were Jennifer Levin's last words?

⇨ *"My bra is killing me!"*

MORE TO COME...

CROTCH ROT

What's the difference between anal sex and a microwave?

⇨ *A microwave won't brown your meat!*

What do gays use condoms for?

⇨ *To pack their lunch!*

What do you do with 365 used condoms?

⇨ *Melt them down into a tire and call it a Good-Year!*

Why do Yuppie women wear leather pants?

⇨ *So their crotches will smell like BMW's!*

What do you call a pervert in the balcony of a porno movie?

⇨ *A tier-jerker!*

MORE TO COME...

BLASPHEMOUS BLASTS

God and Moses were playing a game of golf one day. God tees off, and hits a tremendous shot all the way down the fairway, but it lands about 50 yards short of the hole!

All of a sudden, a squirrel comes running over, picks up the ball with it's mouth, and scampers towards the woods. Just before it reaches there, a hawk comes swooping out of the sky and picks up the squirrel in it's beak and soars off with it, still holding the ball. Then, a bolt of lightening strikes the hawk, knocking the ball out of the squirrel's mouth! The ball bounces once, twice, three times and goes right into the hole!

Moses turns to God and says, "Are we gonna play some golf or are you gonna fuck around all day?"

$$* \quad * \quad *$$

Man: "God, why did you make women so shapely?"
God: "That's so you would like them."
Man: "God, why did you make women so beautiful?"
God: "That's so you would like them."
Man: "But, God, why did you make them so damn
      stupid?"
God: "That's so they would like you!"

$$* \quad * \quad *$$

How do you make Holy Water?
    ⇨ *Take some ordinary water and boil the Hell out of it!*

What do you get when you cross Holy Water with castor oil?

    ⇨ *A religious movement!*

MORE TO COME...

NO 'IFs,' 'ANDs,' OR 'BUTTs,' ABOUT IT!

What did Liberace die from?

⇨ *Botulism! He had bad meat in the can!*

Have you heard Liberace's mother calling him to dinner?

⇨ *YooHoo! Dinner's ready!*
FAAGGGGOOTTTT!"

Did you hear that Rock Hudson's car insurance was cancelled?

⇨ *He kept getting rear-ended!*

Do you know why Rock Hudson's wife threw him out of the house?

⇨ *He kept coming home shit-faced!*

What is a living Hell for a man?

⇨ *Being locked in a room filled with cases of vintage wine and dozens of beautiful women, and all of the bottles have holes in them — and the women don't!*

MORE TO COME...

YUPPIE YUMOR

A Yuppie is involved in a car accident. He is lying in the road, and as the paramedics approach him, they hear him moaning, "Ooooohhhh, my new BMW....oooohhhh, my new BMW..."

One of the paramedics kneels down and tells him, "Look, sir, I don't know if you realize this, but your arm's been torn completely from your body, so I wouldn't worry about the car right now."

The Yuppie looks towards his missing arm and groans, "Ooooohhh, my Rolex...oooohhh, my Rolex."

* * *

What drink do they serve at Drexel-Burnham parties?

⇨ *Subpoena Colladas!*

How do you make $1 million in the stock market?

⇨ *Start with $2 million!*

Did you hear about the stockbroker who used to have a corner on the market?

⇨ *Now he's got a market on the corner!*

More to come...

QUAKE ME WHEN IT'S OVER!

Did you hear about the '89 World Series?
⇨ *San Francisco got rocked!*

Who won?
⇨ *Oakland, by de-fault!*

What was the special event?
⇨ *Helmet Night!*

What were the housing starts in S.F. last month?
⇨ *Flat!*

Did you hear about the 200 gays that got killed?
⇨   *They saw a crack and jumped in!*

MORE TO COME...

CELEBRITY SLEAZE-TAKES!

What did Gary Hart say to Donna Rice?

⇨ *"I told you to 'lick my erection,' not 'wreck my election!'"*

What did Sammy Davis Jr. say to Vanna White?

⇨ *"Gimme an I, please!"*

Why did Liberace play the piano?

⇨ *Cause he sucked on the organ!*

Did you hear that Buckwheat has become a Muslim?

⇨ *He changed his name to Kareem of Wheat!*

Have you seen the new Ronald Reagan typewriters?

⇨ *They've got no memory and no colon!*

MORE TO COME...

CELEBRITY SLEAZE-TAKES!

Why can't Dolly Parton be a schoolteacher?

⇨ *Because every time she turns around, she erases the blackboard!*

What did King Kong say to Oprah Winfrey before her diet?

⇨ *"Is it in?"*

Did you hear about the woman that couldn't decide who to vote for?

⇨ *She wanted Bush in her heart, but Hart in her bush!*

What did George Washington, Thomas Jefferson and Abraham Lincoln have in common?

⇨ *They were the last three white men to have those last names!*

What did Gary Hart have in common with the Challenger space shuttle?

⇨ *They both got blown off the coast of Florida!*

MORE TO COME...

CELEBRITY SLEAZE-TAKES!

What's the difference between Jimmy Swaggert and a pickpocket?

> ⇨ *A pickpocket likes to snatch watches!*

Did you hear about the Jessie Jackson bumper sticker?

> ⇨ *It says, "Run, Jessie, Run," and you put it on the front of the car!*

Do you know why many Blacks won't vote for Jessie?

> ⇨ *Because he's running around promising jobs!*

Did you hear what Jessie said when asked how much he'd be spending on defense?

> ⇨ *He said, "It all depends on how big de-yard is!"*

Did you hear about the movie starring Sylvester Stallone and Rock Hudson?

> ⇨ *It's called "Ram-butt!"*

MORE TO COME...

MORE YUPPIE YUMOR

A woman tells her friend, "I'm married to a stock broker, and an honest guy, too!"

Her friend looks puzzled. She says, "Isn't that bigamy?"

The Devil visits a commodity trader. He says, "Have I got a deal for you! I'll make sure every trade you do in the next ten years is a winner! Every single trade, spreads, outrights, options; everything will make a lot of money. However, after ten years, your mother will die of cancer, your wife will be raped and stabbed, and your children will be kidnaped and slain!"

The trader thinks it over, then asks, "What's the catch?"

After ten years of working at his accounting firm, Horowitz finally gets the key to the men's room. His boss pulls him off to the side to tell him a few secrets.

"On Monday nights, management gets together in the men's room after work and we have a little poker game."

He continues. "On Tuesday nights, we get together in the men's room and blow a little dope. Some of the boys free-base and do some other stuff, but I don't get into that!"

By now, Horowitz looks a little surprised.

"On Wednesdays, the boys get together and we have a couple of really hot-looking hookers come down and they do whatever the hell we ask 'em to do."

Horowitz looks shocked. His boss notices and asks him, "What's the matter, you gay or something?"

Horowitz says, "No, of course not!"

The boss says, "Oh, then you're gonna hate Thursday's!"

More to come...

UNCOMMON SENSE

How do you keep an asshole in suspense?

⇨ *I'll tell you later!*

Why is sex like playing bridge?

⇨ *Because you don't need a partner if you've got a good hand!*

How do you get a woman off your hands?

⇨ *Wash 'em!*

Did I tell ya I had this woman pounding on my door all night last night?

⇨ *Yeah, I finally let her out!*

Did I tell ya my wife ran away with my best friend?

⇨ *Yeah, I really miss him!*

MORE TO COME...

UNCOMMON SENSE

Why is work like a whorehouse?

⇨ *The better you perform, the more you get screwed!*

What's the difference between an oral and a rectal thermometer?

⇨ *The taste!*

What's the difference between worry and panic?

⇨ *Worry is the 1st time you can't do it a 2nd time!
Panic is the 2nd time you can't do it a 1st time!*

How can you tell a second wife?

⇨ *She's the one with the real orgasms and the fake jewelry!*

What's the difference between ooooh and aaaah?

⇨ *About two inches!*

MORE TO COME...

UNCOMMON SENSE

Why do female parachutists always wear tampons?

⇨ *So they don't whistle on the way down!*

What's the difference between the 1980's and the 1960's?

⇨ *In the 80's you walk into a drugstore and say, "(in a bold voice) Hey, gimme a pack of condoms, will ya, (in whisper) and a pack of cigarettes, too!"*

What do you call a Wall Street stock trader?

⇨ *"Waiter!"*

Did you hear that they came out with a deodorant spray for men's genitals?

⇨ *It's called 'Umpire.' Really? Yeah, it's for foul balls!*

Did you hear they have a new perfume for black women only?

⇨ *It's called "Eau de do da day!"*

MORE TO COME...

BALLS TO YOU!

Every Friday, Mrs. Smith, the sixth-grade teacher, asks the class a question at 10 a.m., and anyone who gets it right can go home early and start the weekend! Of course, the catch is that the question is always exceedingly difficult, so no one gets the right answer.

One day, Jimmy has an idea! He goes home Thursday night, and takes out a can of tennis balls and paints them all black. He puts them back in the can and takes it with him to school the next day.

The next morning, it's 10 a.m. and Mrs. Smith says to the class, "O.K., are you ready for your question?"

Just at that moment, Jimmy uncaps the tennis balls and rolls them up toward the front of the room.

The teacher looks down and says, "O.K. who's the comedian with the black balls?"

Jimmy yells out, "Eddie Murphy, teach! See ya Monday!"

*   *   *

MORE TO COME...

BALLS TO YOU, TOO!

Selma's been married to Harry for thirty years. One day, she's cleaning the closet and notices a shoe box in the back. She takes it out and discovers three golf balls and $15,000 in cash! This really upsets her, but she puts the box away and decides not to say anything.

That night while eating dinner, she can't keep it in any longer and says coyly, "You know, I was cleaning the closet today and this shoe box fell on me and three golf balls and $15,000 fell out! Now, you know I trust you Harry, but, I was just curious, a little, so could you tell me how they got there?"

Well, Harry looks ashen-faced. He knows when he's caught and says, "To tell you the truth darling, every time I had an affair I put a golf ball in the shoe box!"

Selma is shocked and can't believe it! But, in thinking it over, she figures, "Thirty years of marriage, three little affairs, it's not the worst thing in the world!"

She says, "Harry, because you've been such a good husband to me, I'm going to forgive you, darling! By the way, what about the $15,000?"

Harry says, "Oh, every time the box got full, I sold them!"

* * *

MORE TO COME...

SOMETHING EVEL COMES THIS WAY!

Did you hear about Evel Knievel's latest stunt?

⇨ *He going to try to drive through Ethiopia with a sandwich on his back!*

Did you hear about the German Evel Knievel?

⇨ *He tried to jump over twelve Jews on a steamroller!*

Did you hear about the Polish Evel Knievel?

⇨ *He tried to jump over twelve motorcycles with a schoolbus!*

What's the Ethiopian National Anthem?

⇨ *"Aren't you hungry?...."*

What do you call a skeleton in a Polish closet?

⇨ *The winner of Hide 'n Seek!*

MORE TO COME...

NASTY KNEE-SLAPPERS!

Why is a blow job like eggs benedict?

⇨ *You can't get either one at home!*

What's the difference between a rectum and an asshole?

⇨ *(Put your arm around a friend and say:) "You can't put your arm around a rectum!"*

What does a hooker say to her customers?

⇨ *"It's been a business doing pleasure with you!"*

Whaddya call a Jewish jerk?

⇨ *A Yidiot!*

Did you hear how Marla Hanson is now billing herself?

⇨ *Actress/Model. (Actress slash model).*

MORE TO COME...

DON'T GET CROSSED WITH ME!

Whaddya get when you cross the Atlantic with the Titanic?

⇨ *About halfway!*

Whaddya get when you cross a piranha with a hooker?

⇨ *Your last blowjob!*

Whaddya get when you cross a vibrator and a groundhog?

⇨ *An armadildo!*

Whaddya get when you cross a lion and a rooster?

⇨ *A lyin' rooster, or a cock you just wouldn't believe!*

Whaddya get when you cross a rooster and a telephone pole?

⇨ *A 25 foot cock that wants to reach out and touch someone!*

MORE TO COME...

QUICKIES

A lady walks into a hardware store. She wants to buy a hinge. The guy behind the counter says, "Hey, lady, do you wanna screw for that hinge?"

She says, "No, but I'll blow ya for the toaster!"

* * *

A lady tells her doctor, "Every time I sneeze, I have an orgasm." He says, "What are you taking for it?" She says, "Pepper!"

* * *

A cowboy walks up to a soda fountain and orders a sundae. The gal behind the counter asks, "Shall I crush your nuts?" He says, "You do and I'll shoot your tits off!"

* * *

A prostitute is being interviewed for a job in a whorehouse. The madame asks her, "Have you ever been picked up by the fuzz?" She says, "No, but I've been swung by the tits a few times!"

* * *

A little boy walks up to a pharmacist and asks, "Mister, do you have cotton balls?" He says, "What do I look like, a teddy bear?"

* * *

MORE TO COME...

WHAT'S DE-MEANING?

What does PTL stand for?

⇨ *Either Part Thy Legs or Pass the Loot!*

What does N.A.A.C.P. stand for?

⇨ *Niggers Are Actually Colored Polacks!*

What does Dwight Gooden think N.A.A.C.P. stands for?

⇨ *Never Admit Any Cocaine Problem.*

What does Pontiac stand for?

⇨ *Poor Ol' Nigger Thinks It's A Cadillac!*

What does N.A.S.A. stand for?

⇨ *Need Another Seven Astronauts!*

What does GAY stand for?

⇨ *Got Aids Yet?*

What does A.I.D.S. stand for?

⇨ *Adios, Infested Dick-Sucker!*

MORE TO COME...

RHYME 'N' SLIME!

Jack and Jill went up the hill,
They each had a quarter.
Jill came down with 50 cents
You think they went up for water!

* * *

Roses are red and are ready for plucking;
Girls out of High School are ready for ...
college!

* * *

Harlem High School Cheer

Watermelons, watermelons
Cadillac car!
We're not as dumb
As you think we is!

SPELLING IT OUT!

How does a Polish couple talk in front of the kids?

⇨ *He says to her, "Let's send the kids to the
M-O-V-I-E-S, so we can stay home and fuck!"*

MORE TO COME...

THE HONEYMOONERS!

What's a honeymoon salad?

⇨ *Lettuce alone without dressing! (Let us alone ...)*

Do you believe in premarital sex?

⇨ *Yes, as long as it doesn't hold up the ceremony!*

Do you smoke after sex?

⇨ *I don't know, I never looked!*

An 85-year-old man marries a beautiful 20-year-old blond bombshell. Hours before he is to leave on his honeymoon, his friend pulls him over to the side and asks, "Tell me, aren't you afraid of a heart attack during sex?

The old man just shrugs it off and says, "If she dies, she dies!"

* * *

MORE TO COME...

A FINE DI-STINK-TION!

What's the difference between looking for a lost golf ball and Lady Godiva?

⇨ *One is a hunt on a course...*

What's the difference between the Miss America pageant and the Superbowl?

⇨ *In the Superbowl they kick a punt...*

What's the difference between Geppetto, Ted Kennedy Jr. and Liberace?

⇨ *One's an old cobbler, one's a bold wobbler and one's a cold gobbler!*

Did you hear the police report after the midget fortune teller broke out of jail?

⇨ *"Be on the lookout for a small medium at large!"*

Did you hear the police report after the cement mixer collided with the paddy-wagon and all the prisoners escaped?

⇨ *"Be on the lookout for twelve hardened criminals!"*

MORE TO COME...

WHERE'S THE BEEF?

Gorbachev is visiting the U.S. and asks President Bush a very special favor.

"Comrade," he says, "in Russia, we have a shortage of what you call, prophylactics. Would you mind if I placed an order for about 100,000 of these things, made to my specifications?"

Bush replied, "No problem, my friend, just let me know what you need!"

So, before Gorby leaves, he tells Bush that he needs 10,000 dozen rubbers, and he wants them to be 3" wide and 18" long! Bush gives the order to a U.S. factory, but tells them, before they are shipped to Russia, there are two things he wants printed on the boxes.

A few days later, the drug company calls him, and says the order is ready and they are awaiting his special instructions.

Bush says, "O.K., on the cover of each box, I want it to say in big, bold letters, MADE IN THE U.S.A.!"

The company exec. says, "O.K., I'll be glad to do that for you; what's the second thing?"

Bush says, "Well under that, I want you to print: Size: Medium!"

More to come...

NO RESPECT!

Picasso shows up at the gates of heaven and says to St. Peter, "Hey, let me in, I'm Picasso!"

St. Peter says, apologetically, "I'm sorry, but I still need to see some I.D."

"Are you kidding, everyone knows who I am!"

"I'm sorry, that is the procedure!"

Picasso says, "Well, I have none on me, how 'bout if I paint something for you?"

St. Peter thinks it over and says, "Well, O.K., I'll get you a canvas."

Picasso paints a fabulous, cubist painting and St. Peter looks at it and says, "Come in, Mr. Picasso!"

A few hours later, Liberace shows up, and St. Peter goes through the same rap with him, insisting on some I.D. Finally, they bring out a piano and Liberace plays some fabulous concertos and St. Peter says, "Come in, Mr. Liberace."

A couple of hours later, Ronald Reagan appears at the gates, asking to be let in. He becomes infuriated when St. Peter asks him for I.D.

St. Peter says, "I'm sorry, Mr. Reagan, but Liberace and Picasso were here earlier today, and I even asked them for I.D."

Reagan looks puzzled and asks, "Who's Liberace and Picasso?"

St. Peter says, "Oh, why come in, Mr. Reagan!"

* * *

More to come...

RAUNCHY RELIGION!

The Pope comes to New York and is driving down Fifth Avenue in an entourage and everyone is yelling and screaming, "We love you Elvis, we love you!"

The Pope thinks, "That's funny, why do they call me Elvis?"

The Pope is now checking into his hotel and people keep passing by him and saying, "We love you, Elvis!"

And the Pope is still wondering why everyone keeps calling him Elvis.

Finally, he gets up to his room, opens the door, and inside is this beautiful, stark-raving naked blonde who screams, "Take me, Elvis, take me!"

The Pope says, "One for the money, two for the show..."

* * *

A priest and a parishioner are playing golf one day, and after the parishioner slices his ball into the woods, he yells, "Goddammit, missed again!"

The priest looks hurt, and warns him, "Son, you shouldn't use the name of the Lord in vain like that. If you continue to do it, you may be struck by lightning!"

The young man apologizes, but on the very next hole, he swings his club at the ball and it just dribbles off to the right, and again he yells, "Goddammit, missed again!"

The priest admonishes him again, warning him that he'll be struck by lightning if he keeps it up.

Well two holes later, the young man hits a ball into the sandtrap, and screams, "Goddammit, missed again!"

All of a sudden, the skies darken. It begins to rain heavily and a giant bolt of lightning comes out of the sky and zaps the priest, turning him into a pile of dust!

A deep voice from the clouds says, "Goddammit, missed again!"

MORE TO COME...

RAUNCHY RELIGION!

Two boys are walking to Catholic school, when one of them gets hit by a car. His friend goes running to school, grabs hold of one of the nuns and says, "Sister, sister, a car hit Joey right in the ass!"

She asks, "Rectum?"

He replies, "Wrecked 'im!?! Damn near killed him!"

HYMN-DINGERS!

A priest is floating in the middle of the ocean after a shipwreck, holding onto nothing but a piece of driftwood. A few hours later, a man in a row boat comes by and offers him help, to which he replies, "No thank you, the Lord will save me!"

A few more hours go by and a man in a canoe rows by and asks the Father if he needs any help. "No thank you," he replies, "the Lord will save me."

Some more time passes by, and a man in a 25-foot cabin cruiser passes by, calling out to the priest, offering help. "It's O.K. my son, the Lord will save me."

The priest drowns! He's up in Heaven and finally gets to meet his maker. "Why didn't you save me?" he asks Him.

"I sent you three fuckin' ships..."

* * *

MORE TO COME...

HYMN-DINGERS!!

Two bums are having a loud argument down on the Bowery, both claiming to be Jesus Christ. They ask a third bum to intervene, and he tells them, "Neither one of you is Jesus Christ...I am...and I can prove it."

They call him to task and he tells them to come with him, over to a nearby saloon. When they walk in, the bartender looks up and says, "Jesus Christ, are you here again?"

* * *

Why is Jesus Christ a lousy lover?
⇨ *Because he's only come once in a thousand years!*

What's the difference between Jesus Christ and an oil painting?
⇨ *It only takes one nail to hang up an oil painting!*

MORE TO COME...

THE DOPE ON THE POPE!

The Pope and the Archbishop were doing a crossword puzzle. The Pope asked the Archbishop, "Monsignor, what is a four-letter word for `woman,' ending with _-U-N-T? He replies, "Well, that would be AUNT, of course!" The Pope asks, "Have you got an eraser?"

* * *

The Pope was feeling a little horny so he found this quiet little room in the back of the Vatican, took out a dirty magazine and started to jerk off! All of a sudden, a tourist stumbles upon him and notices his sinful act! Being from New York, he decides to take advantage of this opportunity! He says, "I'll tell you what, your Holiness, why don't you buy this camera from me, say for $5,000, and I'll forget I ever saw anything!" The Pope exclaims, "Why, this is highway robbery! But, you do have me over a barrel. I guess I'll have to accede to your demands!" So the Pope buys the camera at that extremely exorbitant price.

A few days later, the Pope decides he might as well get some use out of it, so he walks outside and is taking pictures out in the yard when he bumps into the Cardinal. "That's a mighty handsome camera you have there," he says, "Do you mind if I ask you how much you paid for it?" The Pope replies, "Would you believe I paid $5,000 for this?" The Cardinal says, "Boy, somebody must've seen you coming!"

* * *

Three nuns went in to see the Pope, one at a time, and when they got out they started comparing notes.

The first sister says, "Well, when I got in I started looking around, and then, all of a sudden, I looked on his desk and I saw a prophylactic lying there!"

The second sister says, "Yeah, yeah, I saw it, too! And you know what? I took a pin and punched holes in it!"

The third sister fainted!   MORE TO COME...

A SIGN OF THE TIMES

Phil and Jane are getting ready to make it together for the first time in the back seat of his car. She takes off his shirt and notices something surprising.

"How come you have `NIKE' written across your shoulder?"

Phil replies, "Oh, don't mind that. Occasionally I rent myself out as a walking billboard, just to make some extra cash!"

Jane accepts this strange explanation. They continue to make it and when she takes off his pants, she stops again!

"O.K., how come you have `PUMA' written on your leg?"

"I told you...don't worry about it. I'm a walking billboard, just ignore it."

She says, "O.K.," and they continue their passionate pursuits until she takes off his underwear and stops dead in her tracks.

"O.K., I didn't mind it when you had `NIKE' written on your shoulder or `PUMA' written on your leg, but you've got AIDS written on your penis. That's just a little too much."

"Take it easy," Phil snaps back, "in a few minutes, it'll say `ADIDAS!'"

* * *

MORE TO COME...

A SIGN OF THE TIMES!

Tom is taking a vacation in Negril Beach, Jamaica, when he stops at this little shanty on the outskirts of town. He notices a sign outside that says, 'PENIS TATTOOS—$5.' His curiosity has gotten the better of him.

"It's the biggest thing, mon," he is told, "you should try something simple to start, like having your initials tattooed." Tom was kinda drunk at the time, so he thought about it briefly and figured why the hell not.

Later in the day, Tom is back at the resort, and he's taking a leak in the restroom, when a Jamaican comes by and stands in the urinal next to him. Tom was always curious about whether what they say about black people is true, so he couldn't help but peek to see if the man really had larger than average equipment.

"What are you looking at, mon?" the Jamaican asks Tom.

"Oh I'm sorry, I didn't mean to upset you. It's just that I've always been told that black men have larger penises than whites, but I noticed that you just have two initials on yours, `WY,' just like me!" Tom says triumphantly.

"What are you talking about, mon. When I get a hard-on it says, 'WELCOME TO JAMAICA. HAVE A NICE DAY!"

* * *

MORE TO COME...

SMART-ASS KIDS!

A little boy is walking through the streets with his father when all of a sudden, they happen upon two dogs in the act of procreating!

"Daddy, Daddy, what are they doing?"

"Oh, they're making puppies, sonny!"

Later that evening, the little boy can't sleep so he walks into his parents bedroom, and lo and behold, he catches them in the act of making love!

"Daddy, what are you doing!"

"Oh, uh, I'm making you a little brother!"

The kid thinks it over for few minutes, then asks, "Daddy, can you flip'er over? I think I'd rather have a puppy!"

* * *

A little boy walks in on Mom as she is stepping out of the shower. He points right between her legs and asks, "Mommy, what's that?"

She thinks quickly and says, "Oh, uh, that's where God hit me with the golden ax!"

The kid says, "Ooooh! Gotcha right in the cunt, didn't he?"

* * *

A little boy walks into his father's room and sees him holding a prophylactic. He asks him, "What's that, Daddy?"

The father thinks quickly and says, "Err, I'm gonna catch a moth, son!"

The boy says, "What are you gonna do after you catch one? Fuck it?"

MORE TO COME...

MORE QUICKIES

What's long and hard on a black man?

⇨ *Third grade!*

What's white and totally useless on a woman?

⇨ *An Irishman!*

What's twelve inches and white?

⇨ *Nothing!*

What's hard and dry on the way in and soft and sticky when it comes out?

⇨ *Chewing Gum!*

Did you hear about the recent drought in the Midwest?

⇨ *It was so bad the cows were giving powdered milk!*

MORE TO COME...

MORE QUICKIES

A guy walked into the doctor's office, stuck out his nine inch tongue, and the nurse said, "Aaaahhhh!"

* * *

A guy is screwing a hooker and he keeps yelling, "Spread'em wider, spread'em wider!" Finally she says, "Are you trying to get your balls in?" He says, "No, I'm trying to get them out!"

* * *

Have you ever played Howard Beach poker?

⇨ *Three clubs beat two spades!*

A woman calls her chauffeur into her bedroom and says, "Now, James, I want you to take off my blouse! Good! Now, I want you to take off my bra! Good! Now, I want you to take off my panties! Good! And if I catch you wearin 'em again, you're fired!"

* * *

Why is Michael Jackson named Michael Jackson?

⇨ *Because Marvin Gaye was already taken!*

MORE TO COME...

WACKY ONE-LINERS!

What has two gray legs and two brown legs?

⇨ *An elephant with diarrhea!*

Why couldn't the animals on the Ark play cards?

⇨ *'Cause Noah was standing on the deck!*

Why did the Polack marry the dog?

⇨ *Because he had to!*

Two seagulls are flying over Belmont raceway. One of them says to the other, "I'm gonna put everything I have on number 7!"

* * *

A fly spots an attractive female sitting on a piece of manure in the field below. He lands on the piece next to her, and says, "Pardon me, is this stool taken?"

* * *

MORE TO COME...

THE NEW LIGHTBULB JOKES

How many teamsters does it take to change a lightbulb?

⇨ *Twelve...ya gotta problem widdat?*

How many Californians does it take?

⇨ *Five. One to do it and four to share the experience. Or, Californians don't screw in lightbulbs, they screw in hot-tubs!*

How many psychiatrists does it take?

⇨ *It doesn't matter. It won't change unless it wants to change itself!*

How many New Yorkers does it take to change a lightbulb?

⇨ *Go fuck yourself!*

How many Jewish mothers does it take?

⇨ *None, dahling. I'll sit in the dark and suffer!*

MORE TO COME...

YOU MUST BE JOCKING!

"Golden Hands" Johnson, the best-damned receiver in the NFL, is driving his car, when all of a sudden, he spots a big crowd. It seems there's a building on fire, so he pushes his way to the front, and grabs the fire chief and says, "Chief, is there anything I can do?"

He says, "You're `Golden Hands' Johnson, aren't you?"

He says, "Yes, I am, at your service!"

The chief says, "As a matter of fact, the ladder is busted and the net's all worn out and there's a woman up there trapped with her baby. Maybe if she can throw it down and you can catch it..."

"Sure, I can do that, no problem!"

In the meantime, the crowd recognizes him and begins to chant, "Golden Hands, Golden Hands, Golden..."

The chief tries to talk the Mom into dropping her baby down to them. At first, she is reluctant, but finally she agrees, and heaves the baby out the window!

The baby starts to fall to earth, but is taken by a strong gust of wind. Golden Hands starts running as fast as he can, trying to get under the baby. The wind keeps blowing the baby, and Golden Hands keeps chasing it, one block, two blocks, three blocks...

Finally, about four blocks away, Golden Hands runs under the baby and miraculously catches him! He then stops, spins around and instinctively spikes him into the ground!

MORE TO COME...

YOU MUST BE JOCKING!

Three fathers are sitting around bragging about their families. The first one says, "I've got five sons! I've got enough for a basketball team!"

The second one says, "I've got nine sons! I've got enough for a baseball team!"

The third one says, "I've got 18 daughters! I've got enough for a golf course!"

* * *

If athlete's get athletes foot, what do astronauts get?

⇨ *Missile toe!*

Did you hear that the Chicago Bears were attempting to get Lawrence Taylor in a trade?

⇨ *They want to put a coke machine next to the refrigerator!*

What do Lawrence Taylor and Kitty Dukakis have in common?

⇨ *They both blow a little dope!*

What is Bob Ojeda's favorite pitch?

⇨ *The split-fingered fastball! (or the knuckleball)*

MORE TO COME...

YOU MUST BE JOCKING!

Did you hear that the Mets were attempting to trade Bobby O?

⇨ *To Oakland, for Rollie Fingers and a player to be maimed later!*

Did you hear what happened when a reporter tried to interview Bobby O?

⇨ *He gave him the finger!*

What's Dwight Gooden's hardest inning?

⇨ *The last of the eighth!*

What's the Syracuse basketball team's favorite three-point play?

⇨ *Nine foul shots!*

MORE TO COME...

WISE-CRACKS!

What's the difference between a genealogist and a gynecologist?
> ⇨ *One looks up the family tree; the other looks up the family bush!*

A guy in a bar goes up to a woman and says, "You know, I'd love a little pussy!"
> ⇨ *She says, "So would I, mine's as big as a house!"*

A man in a bar says to the bartender, "Hey, Louie, I wanna buy that gal over there a drink, and do me a favor, slip a little Spanish fly into it."

The bartender replies, "I'm sorry, but we're outta Spanish fly. I do have some Jewish fly, though!"

The guy says, "Jewish fly? I never heard of it. Well, O.K., put a little in, will ya?"

The bartender serves the young lady her drink. A few minutes later, she comes over to the guy and says, "Hi, handsome. Wanna take me shopping?"

* * *

Another man in a bar says to the bartender, "Hey, Joe, I wanna buy that douchebag over there a drink!"

The bartender gets pissed. He says, "Don't refer to our customers in that fashion or I'll throw you outta here."

The guy says, "O.K., I'm sorry. It won't happen again. Now, let me just buy her a drink!"

The bartender approaches the woman and tells her, "That fellow over there would like to buy you a drink. What'll it be?"

She replies, "Oh, just give me a vinegar and water, please!"

MORE TO COME...

STROKIN' OFF!

A man is dating Jack Nicklaus' ex-wife, and after a nice, romantic dinner, he takes her back to his hotel room and makes love to her.

A few minutes later, he picks up the phone and says, "I'm going to order some food, what would you like?"

She says, "Oh, Jack wouldn't have done that. Jack would make love to me again!"

So, he hangs up the phone and makes love to her again. Now, near total exhaustion, he picks up the phone again, and says, "What would you like to eat, dear?"

She replies, "Oh, Jack wouldn't eat now. He'd make love to me again!"

He shakes his head in disbelief. He crawls back into the sack and makes love to her once more. After they're done, he gets out of bed and heads toward the phone.

She says, "Who are you calling, room service?"

He says, "No, I'm calling Jack Nicklaus. I want to find out what's par for this hole!"

MORE TO COME...

STROKING OFF!

The Pope and Menachem Begin are golfing one day, when the Israeli Prime Minister happens to mention that they're holding an international golf tournament next month in Tel Aviv. He asked his Holiness, "Would you like to bring a representative?"

"But, of course, we would," the Pope replies, "Thank you for this wonderful opportunity!"

The Pope flies back to the Vatican and calls his old friend, Arnold Palmer, and asks him, "Listen Arnie, I really want to win this tournament, so I'm making you an honorary Cardinal! Would you like to represent us next month in Israel?"

"It would be my pleasure," Palmer says.

A month later, Arnold returns from the big golf match and goes to see his friend, the Pope.

The Pope says, "So, Arnie, may I assume you won the tournament?"

He says, "I'm afraid I have some bad news. I got beat out by one stroke!"

"I don't believe it," said the Pope, dazed. "Who beat you?"

Arnie tells him, "Rabbi Jack Nicklaus!"

* * *

MORE TO COME...

DOWN 'N' DIRTY!

A naive young miss goes to the doctor and asks him shyly, "You know, I'm getting married in two weeks and I don't know a thing about my fiance's private parts! Would you be able to help me?"

"Sure," says the doc, "ask me anything!"

"Well, what's that thing at the end of it called?"

"That's called the `head' or the `glans'!"

"Oh, I see! And how about the thing that it's on?"

"Well, that's known as the rod or the shaft!"

"Oh, thank you! And tell me, doctor, what are those two round things about 14 inches behind the head?"

The doc thinks about it and says, "Ma'am, I don't know about your fiance, but on me it's the cheeks of my ass!"

* * *

A groom and his best man are standing together surveying the entire room, when the groom puts his arm around his old friend and says, "Look around this room! Do you realize, that, except for my sister and my fiance, I've been to bed with every woman here!"

The best man smiles and says, "Well, between the two of us, we got 'em all!"

MORE TO COME...

DOWN 'N DIRTY!

Three sailors and a nurse are shipwrecked on a deserted island. After a few weeks, the nurse finally gives in to the weaknesses of the flesh and begins having sex with all three of them. This goes on for a couple of months but one day, she feels so guilty about it, she kills herself!

The sailors feel so guilty about it, that a few weeks later, they bury the body!

* * *

A man brings his wife a glass of water and two aspirins. She looks surprised and says, "I don't have a headache!"

He says, "Aha!"

* * *

The hunchback of Notre Dame comes home from work one day and sees the Wok out on the kitchen table. He says to his wife, "Chinese food tonight, honey?" She says, "No, I was just ironing your shirts!"

More to come...

CRUDE CRACKS!

During an examination, a proctologist says to his nurse, "Light, please!"

She brings him a beer! He says, "No, I wanted a Butt-Light!"

* * *

Did you hear about the sentimental gynecologist who looked up his old girlfriend?

* * *

Why is your boss like a diaper?

⇨ *'Cause he's always on your ass and he's usually full of crap!*

Why do shepherds like to screw sheep near the edge of a cliff?

⇨ *So they push back harder!*

* * *

Two fleas walk out of a fancy French restaurant in New York. One of them turns to the other and says, "Shall we walk or take a dog?"

* * *

MORE TO COME...

CRUDE CRACKS!

What's the difference between a hormone and a vitamin?

⇨ *You can't make a vitamin! (whore moan.)*

What's the worst thing about our justice system?

⇨ *You're leaving your fate in the hands of 12 people who weren't smart enough to get out of jury duty!*

What do queers and ambulances have in common?

⇨ *You shove a stiff in the back of both of them and they go "weee-oooo-weee-oooo!"*

What lives in the pubic hair of William Bendix?

⇨ *The Lice of Riley!*

What's the difference between a proctologist and a bartender?

⇨ *A proctologist only has to deal with one asshole at a time!*

MORE TO COME...

SHOWSTOPPER!

There's a show that's been on TV for 25 years, and it always starts by picking someone out of the audience to do a knock-knock joke. So, they're having their gala 25th Anniversary show, and the emcee begins by calling up someone from the audience, not realizing he is very drunk and in a surly mood!

"Mr. Peter Jones, begin your knock-knock joke!"
"O.K., knock knock!"
"Who's there?"
"Argo."
"Argo who?"
"Arrr go fuck yourself!"

The audience is in shock! Thousands of people call in complaints to the show and it is immediately cancelled. The host is censured and also suspended.

It is now seven years later. The host is a recovering alcoholic and is attempting to pick up the pieces of his life. He comes to the network with this really revolutionary plan. It seems he has located this computer whiz who has devised a program that can actually screen out all dirty knock-knock jokes. After demonstrating it to the network and the F.C.C., they finally agree to give the show one more chance.

It is the gala opening night for the show. There are

(cont. on next page)

celebrities and well wishers attending from all over the world. The host comes out in his spiffiest tuxedo and announces, "It's time to do the knock-knock joke!"

He chooses a volunteer from the audience. As the man approaches the stage, he can't believe his eyes, but it looks like the same guy from seven years ago. But, he tells himself to stay calm, after all, we now have this new computer safeguard.

"What's your name?"

"Peter Joneshh."

It is him...and he's drunk again!

"O.K., start the knock knock joke."

"Knock knock."

"Who's there?"

"Alabama."

"One moment please." The host fills out `Alabama' on a punchcard and enters it into the computer. Lights are flashing and gears are whirring and finally, minutes later the computer spits out a card. The host reads it: "There are no possible dirty endings to this joke."

Whew! What a relief!

The host says, "O.K., Mr. Jones, you may now tell your knock-knock joke...please take it from the top."

"O.K., knock knock."

"Who's there?"

"Alabama!"

"Alabama who?"

"Arrr go fuck yourself!!"

✳ ✳ ✳

More to come...

FLY THE FIENDLY SKIES

A Polish pilot is pulling into Orly airport for the first time. He looks down below him and remarks to the co-pilot, "Do you believe how short that runway is?"

They circle for a few minutes as the pilot tries to figure out how to land there, and he says again, "I can't believe how short that runway is."

Finally, after 20 minutes, he decides to take a crack at it, and pulls the plane down on the short runway, screeching to a halt just at the edge of the runway!

Once again the pilot says, "I can't believe how short this runway is!"

The co-pilot says, "Yeah, but look at how wide it is!"

* * *

Whaddya get when you cross a Jew with a travel agent?

⇨ *A guilt trip!*

Whaddya get when you cross LSD with a birth control pill?

⇨ *A trip without the kids!*

Why was the rubber flying through the air?

⇨ *It got pissed off!*

MORE TO COME...

EYE DO!

A Polack goes to eye doctor and the Doc pulls out the eye chart. He points to the bottom line:

krycwqcsojmn

He says, "Can you read this?"

The Pole says, "Read it? I know him!"

* * *

A woman goes to the eye doctor and he pulls out the eye chart. He starts at the bottom line.

"Can you see this?

"No."

He goes up one line.

"Can you see this?"

"No."

He goes all the way up to the largest letters.

"Can you see this?"

"No."

Finally, the frustrated doctor whips out his dick and says, "Can you see THIS?"

She says, "That I can see!"

The Doc says, "Aha! You're cock-eyed!"

* * *

A Puerto Rican goes to his very first Yankee game. When he comes back, his family asks him how he enjoyed it. He told them, "It was the most wonderful experience I've ever had! Everyone there was so friendly! As a matter of fact, right before the game started, everyone in the stadium stood up and asked me, `Jose, can you see?'"

MORE TO COME...

LOW BLOWS!

Two peanuts were walking in the park. One of them was a-salted!

* * *

Why is it quiet in New York on Sundays?
>The Jews are visiting their relatives on Long Island.
>The Irish are sleeping off their hangovers.
>The Italians are putting flowers on their relatives' graves.
>The Mexicans can't start their cars.
>The Blacks are in jail.
>The Polacks think it's Tuesday!

* * *

"Your too tense! You're too tense!"
"What are you talking about?"
"Your dick...it's two tense the size of mine!"

* * *

"Have you ever seen the serial number on a prophylactic?"
"No."
"Oh, maybe you've never rolled it back that far?"

MORE TO COME...

LEWD LAFFS!

What's the difference between a fat girl and a virgin?
> *One is trying to diet; the other's dying to try it!*

* * *

A patient is told by his doctor that he needs a urine sample, a stool specimen and a semen sample.

The patient says, "Here, Doc. Take my shorts!"

* * *

Why don't JAPs swallow?
> *They want to be the spitting images of their mothers!*

A woman once told me, "I want you to kiss me where it stinks!" So I drove her to Secaucus!

* * *

Another woman said to me, "I don't want to go to bed with a guy unless he's got a twelve inch cock!"

I said, "I don't cut off two inches for anybody!"

* * *

Yet another woman told me, "I want you to give me nine inches and make it hurt!"

So I fucked her three times and punched her in the mouth!

MORE TO COME...

GET LUCKY!

MAN TO WIFE: "Pack your bags! Pack your bags! I won the lottery!"

WIFE: "Well, should I pack for warm weather or cold?"

MAN: "I don't give a shit! As long as you're outta the house by tonight!"

* * *

Denise comes home wearing this beautiful, new crystal fox coat. Her husband, Bill, looks up and asks, "Honey, where did you get that coat?"

She replies, "Oh, didn't I tell you? I won it in a lottery!"

She takes off the fur and sits down, and Bill notices she's wearing a new emerald bracelet. He asks, "Honey, where did you get that bracelet?"

"Oh, didn't I tell you? I won it in a lottery!"

Later that evening, she yells up to him, "Oh, Billy darling, do you mind drawing up the bath for me?"

"No, not at all darling!"

A few minutes later, she goes into the bathroom, looks into the tub and says, "Oh, Billy, why is there only an inch of water in the tub?"

He yells up, "I thought you only wanted to wet your ticket!"

* * *

A man walks into a whorehouse and lays down two crisp hundred-dollar bills. He says, "I want a girl that's just gonna lay there!"

Surprised, the Madame informs him, "But sir, for $200, you can have the best girl in the house!"

He says, "No, thank you. I'm not horny, I'm just a little homesick!"

MORE TO COME...

A-MEN! (B-WOMEN!)

Why did God invent women?

⇨ *'Cause sheep can't cook!*

Why did God invent alcohol?

⇨ *So fat girls could get laid, too!*

What's the definition of <u>eternity</u>?

⇨ *It's the time between the moment you come and she goes!*

What's the definition of <u>indefinitely</u>?

⇨ *When your balls are slapping against her ass-cheeks, it's in definitely!*

What's the ideal date?

⇨ *A blonde nymphomaniac who turns into a pizza and a six-pack at 1 a.m.!*

MORE TO COME...

BATTLE OF THE SEXES!

MAN: Your box is too tight and your tits are too small.

WOMAN: Get off my back!

* * *

WOMAN: Men are so useless! You've got two balls that don't bounce, a cock that doesn't crow, an ass that can't pull a cart and two tits that don't give milk!

MAN: Look who's talking! You got eggs you can't fry, two lips that can't talk, a pussy that can't catch mice and a period without a sentence!

* * *

Why did God give women a vagina?

⇨ *So men would talk to them!*

Did you hear about the guy who liked to eat his girl right after she douched?

⇨ *He wanted to come up smelling like roses!*

Why are men smarter than women?

⇨ *Because they have two heads!*

MORE TO COME...

BATTLE OF THE SEXES!

Gloria Steinem is on an airplane when all of a sudden, the pilot comes on the loudspeaker, and she is pleasantly surprised to hear a woman's voice! She calls over one of the stewardesses and says, "You know, I'm really impressed with this airline. It's nice to know that there's a woman pilot, for a change."

"Oh, that's nothing," replies the stewardess, "all the other employees are women, too! All the ticket agents, the technicians, all the executives and even the owner is a woman."

"I am so impressed. This is such a thrilling breakthrough for women. Do you think there's any chance that I can meet the owner so that I might congratulate her on this venture?"

"You're in luck. Today's pilot happens to be the owner, too!"

"Do you think you can take me up to the cockpit to meet her?"

"Oh, we don't call it the `cockpit', anymore!"

* * *

Why is a bleached blonde like a 747?

⇨ *They both have black boxes!*

MORE TO COME...

A TIT- FOR -TOT!

Whaddya call snacks for babies?
> ⇨ *Titbits!*

Whaddya call mammary glands that don't work?
> ⇨ *Milk Duds!*

Whaddya call an abortion in Prague?
> ⇨ *A cancelled Czech!*

What did the Puerto Rican fireman name his twin boys?
> ⇨ *Jóse and Jos-B!*

Why should you wash all your clothes in Tide?
> ⇨ *'Cause it's too darn cold out-tide!*

MORE TO COME...

MO AND LESTER!

One child molester to another: "I had this ten-year-old last night; had the body of a six-year-old!"

* * *

What goes into 13 twice?

⇨ *Roman Polanski!*

Did you hear about Polanski's latest film?

⇨ *It's a thriller called, "Fetal Attraction!"*

What's it rated?

⇨ *PG-13; which stands for Polanski goes for 13-year-olds!*

MORE TO COME...

I FORGET THE NAME OF THIS CHAPTER!?!

What's the best thing about Alzheimer's disease?

⇨ *You meet new people everyday!*

Did you hear about the new disease: Waldheimer's?

⇨ *You forget you were a Nazi!*

* * *

A guy goes to the doctor and is told, "I've got some good news and some bad news!"

The guy says, "Better gimme the bad news first."

The Doc says, "The bad news is you've got AIDS!"

"Oh, my God! Quick, gimme the good news!"

"The good news is you've got Alzheimer's also, so go home and forget about it!"

* * *

Patient to Shrink: "Doc, I been losing my memory. What do you suggest I do?"

⇨ *"Pay in advance!"*

MORE TO COME...

WHY DON'T WE DO IT IN THE ROAD?

A man comes across another man lying in the road. He looks up and says, "Mister, call me an ambulance!" The other fellow says, "Are you sure that's what you want?"

He says, "Mister, please, call me an ambulance!"

The other guy says, "O.K., if that's what you want: Hey, mister, YOU'RE AN AMBULANCE!"

* * *

Another man comes across an elderly Jewish man lying in the road. He puts his jacket under his head and says, "Mister, are you comfortable?" The man in the road shrugs and says, "I make a good living!"

* * *

Yet another man is lying in the road who had just been hit by a car and a Jewish man approaches him and says, "Mister, has anyone notified the police?"

He shakes his head, no.

He asks, "Has anyone called an ambulance?"

He shakes his head, NO.

He asks, "Mister, did anyone see the accident?"

He shakes his head, NO.

He asks, "Then, do you mind if I lie down next to you?"

MORE TO COME...

WHY DON'T WE DO IT IN THE ROAD?

A Jewish tank and a Syrian tank are speeding toward each other on a road in the Galilee Mountains. They collide and have a terrible accident. When the dust settles, the Syrians are heard screaming from their tank, "We Surrender! We Surrender!" But the Israeli's don't hear them because they are too busy shouting, "Whiplash! Whiplash!"

OLD JOKES!

A 90-year-old man goes to a hooker. When he gets undressed, she looks at his wrinkled and flaccid penis and says, "Mister, you've had it!"

He says, "Thank you very much. How much do I owe you?"

* * *

ONE OLD MAN TO ANOTHER: "I've got a new hearing aid, now. It cost me a pretty penny, but it's the best one that money can buy!"

FRIEND: "Really, what kind is it?"

OLD MAN: "Oh, it's about a quarter to three!"

* * *

More to come...

OLD JOKES!

An 85-year-old man goes on his honeymoon. He says to his wife, "Honey, I'm going to the bathroom. When I come out, I want you to be ready for me!"

When he comes out of the bathroom, he is surprised to see his new wife standing on her head. He says, "What the hell are you doing?"

She smiles and says, "I figured, if you couldn't get it up, you could drop it in!"

An old man is sitting on the park bench crying. Another old man sits down next to him and says, "Mister, what's the problem?"

The old man wipes the tears from his eyes and explains, "I've got this beautiful, 35-year-old wife, and all she wants to do is make love from the moment I walk in the door till the moment we go to sleep and then when we wake up again."

"So, what the hell is the problem?"

"Mister, you don't understand...I forgot where I live!"

MORE TO COME...

BAGS O' FAGS!

What's the biggest crime of transvestites?

⇨ *Male Fraud!*

Whaddya get when your brother has a sex-change operation?

⇨ *A trans-sister!*

How do birds get AIDS?

⇨ *By kissing a cockatoo! (cock or two).*

What's meaner than a pit bull with AIDS?

⇨ *The guy that gave it to him!*

Did you hear about the gay that was half-Welsh and half-Hungarian?

⇨ *He was Well-Hung!*

MORE TO COME...

HOMO-GENIZED JOKES!

Did you hear about the new gay sitcom?

⇨ *It's called, "Leave it, it's Beaver!"*

* * *

The scene is a Roman orgy. All of a sudden, the Nordic God of War walks in. He announces, "I'm Thor." A voice from the corner yells out, "You're thore, I can hardly pith!"

* * *

Mark Gastineau of the N.Y. Jets is in a bar on Long Island, and he's bragging about his football prowess, when all of a sudden, a little fairy comes up to him and says, "You think you're so good, huh? I invented a game called `Football Drinking,' and I betcha I can beat you at it!"

"Oh, yeah," he replies wittily, "what are the rules?"

"Well, all you have to do is down six straight scotches to score a touchdown, and for the extra point, you have to drop your pants and let out a loud fart!"

Gastineau, who will not be outdone, answers, "You're on, faggot!"

Well, the gay goes first. He has the bartender set up six Scotches for him, downs all of them, then turns around and drops his pants and lets out a loud fart! "Seven to nothing!" he chirps triumphantly.

Now, Gastineau is ready. He tells the bartender to set him up, then he downs six straight Scotches. He drops his pants and bends over to let one rip, revealing his big, hairy ass, when all of a sudden the fag leaps on top of him, jams his cock into his ass and yells, "Block that kick, Block that kick!"

MORE TO COME...

FLAMING FLAMERS!

A burly truck-driver walks into a bar and immediately begins causing trouble.

"Everyone on this side of the bar is a cocksucker," he sneers, looking towards his right. Everyone just sits, mortified.

Then he turns to his left and screams, "Everyone on this side of the bar is a fuckin' asshole!"

A few seconds later, a gay guy gets up and begins walking around the bar.

"Where the hell are you going?" bellows the trucker.

"I mutht be on the wrong thide of the bar," says the flamer!

* * *

Three men in a bar are completely inebriated, when they begin bragging about whose got the biggest cock. "Well, there's only one way to prove it," says one of them. "Let's just take 'em out and lay 'em out right here on the bar and see who's got the biggest!"

The first guy takes his out and lays it across the bar. He's got about six inches.

The next guy says, "I got you beat," takes his out and lays it next to the first guy and sure enough, he's got 'im beat by a good two inches!

The last guy says, "I got ya both beat," and lays his down next to the other two, and it's gotta be at least twelve inches!

Just then, two gay guys walk in, look over towards the bar, and one of them says to the other, "Oh, look, a smorgasbord!"

MORE TO COME...

ON THE DYKE-PIKE!

What's a lesbian?

⇨ *Just another woman trying to do a man's job!*

How can you tell if two lesbians are twins?

⇨ *They lick alike!*

What did one lesbian say to the other?

⇨ *"Your face or mine!"*

What's the beer of lesbians?

⇨ *Busch!*

Did you hear about the Polish lesbian?

⇨ *She likes guys!*

MORE TO COME...

COCKY DOCS!

Doctor: "I've got good news and bad news!"

Patient: "Well, you better give me the good news first."

Doctor: "You've got only twenty-four hours to live!"

Patient: "That's the good news? What the hell is the bad news?"

Doctor: "Oh, I forgot to tell you yesterday!"

* * *

Doctor: "I'm sorry to tell you this, but you've got A.I.D.S.!"

Patient: "What can we do about it?"

Doctor: "Well, I'm gonna put you on a special diet...pizza, matzoh, pancakes..."

Patient: "Will that stuff help me?"

Doctor: "No, but that's the shit we can easily slip under the door...!"

* * *

Doctor: "I'm sorry to tell you, but you've got just six months to live!"

Patient: "What can I do about it?"

Doctor: "Well, I suggest you marry a J.A.P. and move to the suburbs..."

Patient: "Will that help me live longer?"

Doctor: "No, but it'll make the six months seem like an eternity!"

MORE TO COME...

COCKY DOCS!

Doctor to Old Man: "Do you have trouble urinating?"
Old Man: I urinate, like clockwork, at exactly 8 a.m.!"
Doctor: "What about bowel movements?"
Old Man: "Every morning for the past 70 years, at exactly 9 a.m., knock on wood, I move my bowels!"
Doctor: "That's wonderful! Then, what seems to be the problem?"
Old Man: "I don't get up til 10!"

* * *

A man walks into a doctor's office and announces, "I'm having a lot of trouble with my penis." The receptionist becomes shaken up and runs out of the office. The doctor pulls the man aside and says to him, "What's the matter with you? You don't say something like that! First you tell her you have some other problem, then when you come in to see me, you tell me all about the real problem!

About a week later, the same man walks in, and this time he announces, "I'm having trouble with my finger." The receptionist asks him, "What seems to be the problem?" He says, "I can't pee through it!"

* * *

Woman: "Doctor, the strangest thing has been happening to me. Last week, some quarters fell out of my vagina. A few days later, some nickels and dimes fell out. Then this morning I found some pennies in my underwear!"
Doctor: "Relax, you're just going through your change!"

MORE TO COME...

THE DICK DOCTOR!

A man walks into a doctor's office and proclaims, "D-d-d-doc, I-I-I h-h-have this r-r-really b-bad p-p-problem. I-I h-h-h-have t-trouble t-t-talking a-and m-my w-w-wife i-is th-th-th-threatening to l-leave m-me if I-I-I d-d-don't d-do s-s-something about i-it!"

The doctor tells him, "Well, take off all your clothing and let me give you an examination!"

The guy gets undressed. The doctor takes one look at him and gasps! His shlong is almost hanging down to the floor!

The doctor says, "Your problem is obvious! Your penis is so large that it's exerting downward pressure on all your internal organs. Because of this, your vocal cords are being tugged on, and that's what's causing you to stutter! All I have to do is remove your penis and put back a smaller one, and all your problems will be solved!"

The guy says, "W-w-well, l-l-let's d-do it r-right a-away, m-my w-wife's b-been g-getting r-really i-impatient."

The doctor performs the operation; then the man thanks him and leaves.

About two weeks later, there's a knock on the door and the doctor is very surprised to see that it's the same guy! He opens the door and the guy says, "Doc, I really gotta hand it to you. You are some kind of genius! I never believed I could sound like this! But, you're not gonna believe this. My wife kinda misses the old me, if you know what I mean! I can't satisfy her in bed anymore! So, if you don't mind, we decided to have another operation and have my old penis put back! Will ya do it for me, Doc?"

The doctor says, "I-I-I'm s-s-s-sorry! I-I-I c-c-can't..."

MORE TO COME...

DICKS OR DOCS?

Did you hear that they now say you can get A.I.D.S. from a mosquito?
> ⇨ *Well, I say, anyone who's sick enough to fuck a mosquito, deserves it!*

* * *

Gynecologist (examining woman): "What a hole! What a hole!"

Woman: "I know it's large; you didn't have to say it twice!"

Gynecologist: "I didn't, that was an echo!"

* * *

Doctor: "Hey, lady, you really smell bad! You oughtta take a shower!"

Woman: "That's what the last doctor told me!"

Doctor: "So, why didn't you listen?"

Woman: "Well, I wanted to get a second opinion!"

* * *

Did you hear about the deaf gynecologist?
> ⇨ *He had to learn how to read lips!*

Do you know why the gynecologist's wife left him?
> ⇨ *She found out he was seeing other women!*

MORE TO COME...

DORKS OR DICKS?

Gynecologist (to an elderly Jewish patient):
"Pardon me for saying so, ma'am, but you have
the cleanest vagina I've ever seen!"
Woman: "Vell, it should be clean. I have a
<u>shvartze</u> come in twice a week!"

* * *

A doctor and nurse are making the rounds on a
hospital floor, taking all the patients'
temperatures and recording them.

"Thermometer, please," he asks the nurse, and
inserts it rectally.

They walk to the next bed, where he says,
"Pen, please," and he records the previous
patient's temperature.

They continue this procedure.

"Thermometer, please." "Thank you."

"Pen, please." "Thank you."

"Thermometer, please." "Thank you."

"Pen, please." And she hands him the
thermometer!

The Doc says, "Uh, oh! Some asshole's got my
pen!"

* * *

Did you hear what happened during Nancy
Reagan's mastectomy?

⇨ *They removed the wrong boob from the White
House!*

MORE TO COME...

DORKS OR DICKS?

What's a Jewish phrase for Prince, beginning with an "A?"

⇨ *A doctor!*

* * *

A man is told by his doctor that he's got AIDS!
"Oh, my God, Doc, what should I do?"
"Well, I suggest you go to every Indian restaurant in New York, order the curry and eat as much of it as you can!"
"Really, will that help?"
"No, but it'll give you a fuckin' good idea of what your asshole's <u>supposed</u> to be used for!"

* * *

Doc: "I've got good news and bad."
Patient: "What's the bad news?"
Doc: "The bad news is you've got six months to live!"
Patient: "Oh my God! Quick, give me the good news."
Doc: "Well, did you notice the receptionist out there?"
Patient: "Yeah."
Doc: "The one with the big boobs and the gorgeous legs?"
Patient: "Yeah, yeah?"
Doc: "The one with the silky blonde hair and the beautiful sensuous lips?"
Patient: "Yeah, yeah, tell me, tell me!"
Doc: "Well, I'm fuckin' her!"

MORE TO COME...

KINKY KARS!

What car do winos drive?

⇨ *Thunderbirds!*

What do chickens drive?

⇨ *Coupes!*

What do purse-snatchers drive?

⇨ *The Sprint!*

What does Prince Charming drive?

⇨ *A Valiant!*

What are the three French words all Black people know?

⇨ *Coup De Ville!*

MORE TO COME...

KINKY KARS!

What car does a hooker drive?

⇨ *An Escort!*

What cars do Rabbis prefer not to drive?

⇨ *Christ-lers!*

What about Fred the Furrier?

⇨ *A Lynx or a Sable!*

How about Robin Leach?

⇨ *The Celebrity!*

And the baker?

⇨ *A Rolls!*

MORE TO COME...

KINKY KARS!

What car does Nixon drive?

⇨ *The Bug!*

What car does Robert Blake drive?

⇨ *The Baretta!*

What does the Mayor drive?

⇨ *A Civic!*

And an airplane pilot?

⇨ *A Delta 88!*

How 'bout a bullfighter?

⇨ *The Toro!*

MORE TO COME...

KINKY KARS!

What car do Jews drive?

⇨ *Hondels!*

What do golfers drive?

⇨ *Caddies!*

What do depressed people drive?

⇨ *Saabs! (sobs.)*

What do senior citizens drive?

⇨ *Olds!*

What car do cops drive?

⇨ *Citations!*

MORE TO COME...

KINKY KARS!

What car do Indians drive?

⇨ *A Cherokee!*

What cars do the French drive?

⇨ *Coup De Villes!*

What about jet-setters?

⇨ *The Riviera!*

And a scuba diver?

⇨ *The Benz!*

How about an Ambassador?

⇨ *The Diplomat!*

MORE TO COME...

KINKY KARS!

Which cars do Libyans stay away from?

⇨ *American Motors cars!*

What car do tax evaders drive?

⇨ *The Dodge!*

And how about a symphony orchestra conductor?

⇨ *The Prelude!*

What does Hayley Mills drive?

⇨ *Hayley's Comet*

What do astronomers drive?

⇨ *Novas!*

MORE TO COME...

KINKY KARS!

What car does Elvis drive?

⇨ *The Legend!*

What car do weather-people drive?

⇨ *Mercurys!*

What would you drive on an Easter Sunday?

⇨ *A Rabbit!*

What car would a bandleader drive?

⇨ *A Tempo!*

What cars do bond traders drive?

⇨ *Convertibles!*

MORE TO COME...

SHOPPING MAULS!

Where do midgets shop?

⇨ *In Bergdwarfs!*

Where do people with no arms and legs shop?

⇨ *In Saks!*

Where do people with a wooden leg shop?

⇨ *In Gimpels!*

Where do they eat breakfast?

⇨ *At I.H.O.P.s!*

Where do dead people shop?

⇨ *Nieman Carcas!*

What do they buy there?

⇨ *Cadaver Chocolates!*

MORE TO COME...

SHOPPING MAULS!

Where do gay people shop?

⇨ *A & Asses!*

Where do Polacks shop?

⇨ *Dimwit Teller's!*

Where do Black people shop?

⇨ *F.A.O. Schvartze!*

Where do slaves shop?

⇨ *In chain stores!*

Where do the Irish shop?

⇨ *At Blarnie's!*

Where do rats shop?

⇨ *R.H. Mazey's!*

MORE TO COME...

SHOPPING MAULS!

Where do Southerners shop?

⇨ *KKK-Mart!*

Where do child molesters shop?

⇨ *Boys-R-Us!*

Where do fat people invest money?

⇨ *E.F. Glutton!*

Where does Peter Pan eat?

⇨ *Wendy's!*

What do Jews drink on holidays?

⇨ *Chivous Regal!*

Where do thieves shop?

⇨ *Crooks Bros.!*

MORE TO COME...

DIZZNY CHARACTERS

What did Donald Duck say to the hooker?

⇨ *Put it on my bill!"*

What part of Popeye never gets rusty?

⇨ *The part he keeps in Olive Oil!*

What's red and has seven dents?

⇨ *Snow White's cherry!*

How does Snow White get seven inches?

⇨ *An inch at a time!*

✳ ✳ ✳

The judge at Mickey Mouse's divorce proceedings pulls him into his chambers and says, "I just had a long talk with Minnie, and she doesn't seem stupid to me!"

Mickey replies, exasperated, "I didn't say she was stupid, your Honor! I said she was fucking Goofy!"

MORE TO COME...

ANIMAL KINKDOM!

Two fleas are lying next to each other on the beach in Fort Lauderdale and one of them notices the other one is shivering and under a blanket.

He says, "Excuse me, I don't mean to be rude, but are you O.K.?"

He says, "Yeah, I'll be O.K., you see I came down on a biker's beard so I'm just a little cold right now from the ride!"

The other flea says, "I don't mean to be pushy, but what you should do is find yourself a nice, warm snatch and climb aboard! That's the way I do it!"

A year passes and the flea goes back to the same beach and sure enough he spots his friend again, but much to his surprise, he is shaking and under a blanket again!

He flies over and asks, "Hey, what happened? I thought you were going to take my advice?"

He says, "I did, I found myself this beautiful, warm snatch and climbed aboard, then the next thing I knew, I was back on the biker's beard again!"

* * *

What's the fastest animal in the world?

⇨ *The Ethiopian chicken!*

MORE TO COME...

ANIMAL KINKDOM!

A man walks into a Baltimore bar with his dog and asks the bartender, "Do you mind putting on the Orioles game? My dog happens to lllove the Orioles!"

The bartender says, "Why not?" and puts on the game.

In the top of the third inning, the Orioles string together two walks and a throwing error and take the lead, 1-0. The dog is leaping into the air, and barking and wagging it's tail frantically.

In the top of the ninth, the Orioles come up with another run on an infield single, a stolen base, a ground-out and a walk. Again, the dog begins leaping into the air, barking and going crazy.

But, alas, in the bottom of the ninth, the Orioles give up a three-run homer and they lose the game. The dog begins yelping and whining and rolling around on the ground and running into the wall. The bartender can't believe it. He asks the man, "Boy, I can't believe how upset he gets. What the hell does he do when they win?"

The man replies, "Oh, I don't know! I only have him two years!"

* * *

MORE TO COME...

ANIMAL KINKDOM!

Why did the bee wear a yarmulka?

⇨ *He didn't want to be mistaken for a wasp!*

What did the elephant say to the naked man?

⇨ *"How do you eat with that thing?"*

What do you do with an elephant with three balls?

⇨ *Walk him and pitch to the giraffe!*

Why does an elephant have four feet?

⇨ *He'd look silly with six inches, wouldn't he?*

MORE TO COME...

WHADDYA CALL?

Whaddya call a hernia on a walrus?
⇨ *A Loose-seal Ball!*

Whaddya call a Jewish eskimo?
⇨ *Iceberg!*

Whaddya call a black hitchhiker?
⇨ *Stranded!*

Whaddya call a Puerto Rican with no arms and legs?
⇨ *Trustworthy!*

What do you call a Black man who graduated from Yale, went on to receive a Harvard MBA and earns one million dollars a year on Wall Street?
⇨ *Nigger!*

MORE TO COME...

MINORITY CRACKS!

Three Italians and three Polacks are working in a factory and while eating lunch, they all decide that they're fed up with the place. One of the Italians comes up with an idea!

He says, "I got it! When the boss comes in, we'll do something really crazy. He'll fire us and then we don't have to work here anymore!"

So the men go back to work and when they see the boss coming, the three Italians climb up onto the rafters and hang upside down from them!

The boss looks up at them and says, "What the hell are you guys doing?"

They answer, "We're lightbulbs!"

The boss says, "You Guineas are crazy. You're fired!"

The three guys climb down from the rafters and walk out.

The boss turns around and sees the three Polish guys leaving. He says, "Where the hell are you Polacks going?"

They say, "We can't work in the dark!"

* * *

More to come...

MINORITY CRACKS!

A man finds a brass bottle on the beach. He rubs it and a genie pops out! She says, "I'll grant you three wishes, but there's a catch. Everything you ask for, no matter what it is, every Black person in the world will get twice as much or twice as many!"

The guy thinks it over and says, "O.K., for my first wish, I want $10 million!"

She says, "O.K., you got it, but remember, every Black in the world now has $20 million!"

He says, "O.K., for my next wish, I want a Rolls Royce!"

She says, "O.K., you got it, but remember, every Black in the world now has two Rolls!"

The man shrugs. He says, "O.K., I want you to listen to me very carefully now. For my third wish, I want you to choke me half to death!"

MORE TO COME...

BLACCENTS!

A man walks up to another man on the street and says, "I'll betcha $10 I can make you cry?"

The man looks at him increduously, and says, "You got yourself a bet!"

So the first guy says, "O.K., knock knock."

"Who's there?"

"Boo."

"Boo who?"

"See, I made you cry," and he grabs the ten bucks and runs!

Now, this man who lost the bet feels really stupid and he tells himself, "I gotta get my money back!"

So, he goes up to this black guy on the street, and says, "Hey, bro, I'll betcha $10 I can make you cry!"

The black dude thinks about it and replies, "O.K., my man, you got a bet!"

The white guy starts, "Knock knock!"

"Who's there?"

"Boo."

"Who be Boo?"

* * *

"Do Black people talk funny?"

⇨ "No, it be a miff!"

MORE TO COME...

BLACCENTS!

A man calls the NAACP and says, "Put the head nigger on, please!"

The man on the phone, who happens to be the president of the chapter, says, "Pardon me, but what did you say?"

He repeats, "I'd like to talk to the head nigger!"

The Black man says irately, "Do you happen to know who you're speaking to?"

The man says, "Look, I got $100,000 I want to contribute to your organization. Can you please put the head nigger on?"

He replies, "Hang on, ya'all, I thinks I sees that jigaboo comin' down da hall right now!"

* * *

A woman walks into a bar and orders a beer.

The bartender asks her, "Anheiser-Busch?"

She says, "Fine, and how's your cock?"

* * *

A man walks into a bank and says to the teller, "Listen, bitch, I wanna open up an account!"

She says, "What did you say?"

He says, "What are you, deaf, slut? I wanna open up an account!"

She goes running off to the manager, crying. He comes up to the window himself and says to the man, "Excuse me, but can you repeat what you just said?"

The guy says, "Look, I told that stupid whore that I wanna open an account. I've got $100,000 in this bag and I'd like to stick it in the bank!"

The manager says, "And that cunt was giving you a hard time?"

MORE TO COME...

BLACCENTS!

Did you hear about the Black guy who had nothing to wear for Halloween, so he went completely naked wearing only a pair of roller skates and told everybody he was dressed as a pull toy?

* * *

Did you hear about the Black dude who didn't have a Halloween costume so he threw his shlong over his shoulder and went as a gas pump?

* * *

Did you hear about the two Black women who bump into each other in the supermarket and one says to the other, "So how's ya'all been, honey child? I's hasn't seen you in ages!"

She replies, "Well, well, dere's so much news to tell ya'all. Ya know I's married now!"

Her friend replies, "Married? I's didn't even know you was pregnant!"

* * *

Two other Black women bump into each other in the supermarket, and one tells the other, "Well, I have sixteen children now. But I did something that was real smart. I named all of them Leroy, so when I want 'em to come to dinner, all I have to do is yell, `Hey, Leroy, come to dinner,' and they all come, or I say, `Hey, Leroy, get in the car,' and they all get into the car!"

Her friend stops her and asks, "But, wait a minute. What happens when you only want one of them?"

Her friend smiles and says, "Oh, then I call 'im by his last name!"

More to come...

SPICY SPORTS

What does Gary Carter have in common with Cat Stevens?

⇨ *Neither one has had a hit in years!*

* * *

Pietro is an Italian man living in Bay Ridge who is visited by his mother from Italy. She has heard a lot about baseball in Italy, especially about the living legend, Joe DiMaggio. So, Pietro promises to take his Mom to a Yankee game.

There they are at Yankee Stadium and finally, Joe DiMaggio steps up to the plate.

"Ball 1," says the umpire.

"Ball 2," he calls the next one.

"Ball 3."

"Ball 4!"

Joe begins to trot down to first base. Pietro's mother stands up and yells, "Run, Joe, run!"

Pietro quickly explains, "He can't run, Mom, he's got four balls!"

She says, "Oh! Then walk-a proud, Joe, walk-a proud!"

* * *

What do the Chicago Bears and Chicago White Sox have in common?

⇨ *They both win once a week!*

MORE TO COME...

TASTELESS!

Did you hear the one about the farmer's daughter who couldn't keep her calves together?

* * *

How about the one about the nurse who hated boating, but liked to go down on the dock?

* * *

A traveling salesman's car breaks down, and he walks over to a nearby farm. He knocks on the door and the farmer appears.

"Excuse me sir, but my car broke down about a mile down the road, and I was wondering if you had a place I could stay, just until morning, and I ..."

The farmer says, "Well, I can let you sleep in the barn, but you'll have to sleep with my two sons..."

The salesman says, "Sons! I must be in the wrong joke!"

* * *

A lady wants to buy a baseball bat. The guy behind the counter says, "Hey, lady, you wanna ball for that bat?"

She says, "No, but I'll blow you for the skateboard!"

* * *

MORE TO COME...

TASTELESS!

What's the difference between a hobo and a homo?

⇨ *A hobo has no friends. A homo has friends up the ass!*

When was Hitler in his worst mood?

⇨ *When he got the gas bill!*

What did Hitler tell himself in heaven?

⇨ *"Next time, no more Mr. Nice Guy!"*

What beverage was served on the Titanic?

⇨ *Sanka!*

How can you tell if a guy is sadistic?

⇨ *He likes to beat around the bush!*

MORE TO COME...

TASTELESS!

A distraught young woman enters a super-strict monastery where the rules are you cannot speak at all, except that every ten years, you receive a review and you're allowed to say two words!

After ten long years, the young woman is finally called in for her review. The Mother Superior opens her files and says, "Sister Maria, you have put in ten years of hard work and we are very pleased with you. Is there anything you have to say at this point?"

She says, "Bed hard."

The Mother replies, "We shall see what we can do!"

Ten more years go by and the Sister is called in for her review. The Mother Superior says, "Sister Maria, we are very pleased with your work here, so far. Is there anything that you want to say at this point?"

She says, "Food cold."

The Mother replies, "We shall see what we can do!"

Another ten years goes by and she is again called for her review. The Mother Superior says, "You have done excellent work here so far. Is there anything you want to say at this point?"

She says, "I quit!"

The Mother Superior remarks, "I'm not surprised. You've been here thirty years and you haven't stopped bitching and moaning..."

* * *

MORE TO COME...

TASTELESS!

Superman has had a bad case of the hots for Wonder Woman for many years, and one day, he's flying over a field and sees her lying there, stark raving naked with her legs spread wide open and her hip gyrating into the air! Without a moment's hesitation, he swoops in, takes out his Super-thing and rams it into her, pumping wildly for hours and hours. Finally, when it's completely finished, he rolls over and asks her, "How was it for you, Wonder Woman?"

She says, "Oh, for me it was great. I just wonder if the Invisible Man will ever be able to walk again!"

* * *

Do you know what the three degrees stand for in college?

B.S. means "Bullshit."

M.S. means "More Shit."

Ph.D. means "Piled Higher and Deeper."

* * *

MORE TO COME...

TASTELESS!

A man walks up to a woman in a bar and says, "If I said I would pay you $1 million to go to bed with me, would you do it?"

She thinks it over and says, "Yeah, I guess I would!"

Then he says, "Would you go to bed with me for $50?"

She slaps his face and says, "What kind of girl do you think I am?"

He says, "We already established that. Now we're just negotiating the price!"

* * *

An elderly man walks into a whorehouse in Israel and asks to see Becky. The madame informs him, "Becky happens to be our most expensive girl. She's $100 per hour."

He says, "That's okay, I want to see Becky!"

He goes in to see Becky and has the time of his life, after which he pays her $100.

He comes back the next day and asks to see her again. As a matter of fact, he comes back every day that week, and goes through the same routine each day. After his final visit on Friday, they're sitting around talking and Becky asks him, "So, where are you from?"

He says, "I'm from Flatbush Avenue in Brooklyn!"

She says, "I don't believe it! I have a friend who lives on Flatbush Avenue! His name is Seymour Goldberg. Do you know him?"

"Of course, I know Seymour. He's a very good friend of mine. As a matter of fact, he gave me $500 to give to you!"

MORE TO COME...

TASTELESS!

A man and his wife are discussing the kids one morning and they both agree that they've been cursing too much. The husband tells the wife to start putting her foot down starting with breakfast, and he goes off to work.

She comes down to the breakfast table and the kids are waiting there. She says to the first one, "O.K., what do you want for breakfast?"

He replies, "Just gimme some goddamn corn flakes!"

She leaps across the table and knocks him off his chair. She grabs him by the collar and smacks him in the face a few times, then drops him on the floor and kicks him in the back, for good measure.

She then turns to the other kid and says, "And what do you want for breakfast?"

The kid says, "Well, I sure as shit don't want no fuckin' corn flakes!"

* * *

MORE TO COME...

TASTELESS!

Three friends die in a car accident and they find themselves at the gates of heaven, awaiting their fate.

The first one is told to enter the room on the right, and a few minutes later, a really ugly girl walks in, with warts all over her face and disgusting scars and moles all over her body. And a deep voice says, "Gary, you have sinned. You must now spend all of eternity with this hideous creature."

The second friend is told to enter the room on the right and a few minutes later, another incredibly ugly girl comes in, and the voice says, "Harry, you have sinned. You must now spend all of eternity with this hideous creature!"

The third friend is told to enter the last room. He waits a few minutes, and the door opens and in walks Bo Derek! He can't believe it! Then, a voice says, "Bo Derek, you have sinned..."

MORE TO COME...

TASTELESS AND GROSS!

What's the difference between a pussy and a cunt?

⇨ *A pussy is warm, moist and soft and a cunt is the person who owns it!*

What's the difference between erotic and kinky?

⇨ *Erotic is when you use a feather and kinky is when you use the whole chicken!*

Whaddya do when an elephant comes in your window?

⇨ *Swim!*

Whaddya have when you have two green balls in your hand?

⇨ *Kermit the Frog's undivided attention!*

What do a hurricane, a tornado, a fire and a divorce have in common?

⇨ *They are four ways you can lose your house!*

MORE TO COME...

TASTELESS AND GROSS!

A man is approached by a hooker who asks him, "Would you like to take me out?"

The man says, "I have three good reasons why I can't!"

The hooker asks, "What are they?"

The man says, "Well, first of all, I don't have the money."

She says, "Shove the other two up your ass!"

* * *

A man approaches a hooker and asks, "How much?"

She says, "$250."

He says, "Don't you think that's a little expensive?"

She says, "Yes, but I'll do anything you want; anything at all!"

The man thinks it over, then gives her the money and says, "O.K., bitch, now paint my house!"

* * *

A man walks up to a woman in a bar and starts to whisper sexy things into her ear. After a few minutes, she turns to him and says, "Listen, I think it's only fair to tell you that I'm a lesbian!"

The man looks at her and says, "What's a lesbian?"

She looks at him and sees that he is serious. She says, "Well, you see that brunette over there at the end of the bar. Well, right now, I wish my head was between her legs, nibbling on her juicy muff pie."

The man sits back, and then begins crying. She asks him, "What's the matter?"

He blurts out, "I think I'm a lesbian!"

MORE TO COME...

LOOK OUT BELOW!

How many successful jumps does it take to make the Skydivers Club?

⇨ *All of them!*

* * *

A guy is ready to make a head-first parachute jump when the instructor comes over to give some last-minute advice. He says, "Remember, wait about one minute, then open your chute. If that one doesn't open, wait until you're about 500 feet from the ground, and open your emergency chute. Remember, there'll be a truck down there waiting for you when you land, to take you back to the school."

The guy jumps. He waits a minute and opens his chute...nothing happens. He waits a few more minutes, and now that he can see the ground, he opens his emergency chute...nothing happens! As he's plummeting to earth, he thinks to himself, "There's probably no damn truck, either!"

* * *

A guy is parachuting down to earth and he begins to plummet because there's a hole in his chute! He pops open the emergency chute but that becomes entangled with the first chute and now he's really in deep shit. All of a sudden, he sees a guy flying up towards him, through the sky! As he passes, he yells, "Hey, do you know anything about parachuting?"

The guy answers, "No, do you know anything about steam boilers?"

MORE TO COME...

FREAKIN' RICANS!

What are the first four English words a Puerto Rican learns?

⇨ *"Attention all K-Mart shoppers!"*

Whaddya call two Puerto Ricans playing basketball?

⇨ *Juan on Juan!*

Why do they spread shit on the floor at a Puerto Rican wedding?

⇨ *To keep the flies off the bride!*

Whaddya call a Puerto Rican in a three-piece suit?

⇨ *Defendant!*

Whaddya call a Puerto Rican with a Spaniard?

⇨ *Spic 'n Span!*

MORE TO COME...

SAY WHA'?

What does a gynecologist say when he comes home from work?

⇨ *"Honey, I'm bushed!"*

What does a Southern Jew say?

⇨ *"Chai, ya' all!"*

What do you call two people making love in a sports car?

⇨ *Handicapped porking!*

What does a gay guy say in a bar?

⇨ *"Can I push your stool in for you?"*

Stewardess to gentleman on plane: "Would you like some TWA coffee, TWA soda, or TWA wine?"

⇨ *Gentleman: "No, but I would like some TWA Tea!"*

MORE TO COME...

JUNGLE BUNNIES!

If Tarzan and Jane were Jewish, what would Cheetah be?

⇨ *A fur coat!*

If Tarzan and Jane were Italian, what would Cheetah be?

⇨ *The guy's sister!*

If Tarzan and Jane were Puerto Rican, what would Cheetah be?

⇨ *The other woman!*

If Tarzan and Jane were Polish, what would Cheetah be?

⇨ *The brains of the family!*

If Tarzan and Jane were Persian, what would Cheetah be?

⇨ *Their rug!*

MORE TO COME...

STRANGE BUT TRUE!

What's the first three words in a Puerto Rican cookbook?
> ⇨ *Steal three eggs...*

What's the first four words of an article describing an Irish social event?
> ⇨ *"Among the injured were..."*

* * *

A teacher is showing the class pictures and asking the children to identify with them.
"Now, can anyone tell me what this is?"
"Linda?"
"That's a rake, teacher."
"Very good Linda. Now here's the next picture. Can anyone identify this picture?"
Nobody answers. "Nobody knows? Well, this is a hoe."
Little Johnny raises his hand. He says, "No, it's not, teacher!"
She asks, "Why do you say that, Johnny?"
He says, "Cause my sister's a hoe, and she don't look nothin' like that!"

* * *

A man enters a fortune teller's tent at a carnival and asks, "How much do you charge?"
She replies, "$50.00 for two questions."
He pays her the money and asks, "Don't you think $50.00 for two questions is pretty steep?"
She answers, "Yes, what's your second question?"

MORE TO COME...

ETHNICS OVER EASY

A Polish fellow and his Czechoslovakian friend sneak into the Bronx Zoo after it is closed. They climb over a fence, whereupon they are discovered by a male and female polar bear, and are promptly devoured.

The next day, foul play is suspected so the police and medics are summoned to the bear's cage. They shoot both bears, cut open the female and find the remains of the Polish fellow.

"Uh, oh," says the zookeeper, "that means the Czech is in the male!"

* * *

Two Polish heroin addicts are shooting up, when one turns to the other and says, "You better not use my needle, you might get A.I.D.S."

The other fellow laughs. "Don't worry! I'm wearing a rubber!"

* * *

Why don't Ethiopians go to the movies?

⇨ *They can't keep the seats down!*

What are the two most commonly told Polish lies?

⇨ *"The check is in your mouth," and "I won't come in the mail!"*

MORE TO COME...

ETHNICS OVER EASY!

How does a J.A.P. get a Ph.D.?

⇨ *She marries him!*

Why do Jews wear yarmulkas?

⇨ *Because it cost extra for the mouse ears!*

Why do Jewish men die before their wives?

⇨ *Because they want to!*

Why is a Jewish divorce so expensive?

⇨ *Because it's worth it!*

Have you seen that Jewish porno movie?

⇨ *"Debbie Does Dishes!"*

MORE TO COME...

ETHNICS OVER EASY!

Jessie Jackson arrives at the gates of heaven and asks to be let in. St. Peter asks him, "Well, can you tell me some of your accomplishments while down on earth?"

Jessie says, "Well, I was a reverend while I was down there!"

St. Peter says, "Well, there were a lot of reverends you know!"

Jessie says, "Well, I was a politician and a leader of my people!"

St. Peter smiles and says, "There were a lot of politicians and a lot of leaders!"

Jessie smiles and says, "I became the first Black President of the United States!"

St. Peter finally looked impressed. He says, "Really, when did this happen?"

Jessie says, looking at his watch, "Oh, about ten minutes ago!"

* * *

A Polack, an Italian and a Black all go to heaven. While they are up there, the Polack goes up to God and asks him, "Lord, will there ever be a Polish President?"

God says, "Why, sure there'll be. In the not too distant future."

The Italian then asks God, "Will there ever be an Italian President?"

And God replies, "Why sure there'll be; not too soon, but sometime down the line!"

And the Black guy goes up to God and asks, "Lord, will there ever be a Black President?"

And God answers, "I'm sure there will be; not in my lifetime, but..."

MORE TO COME...

☞

PATHETIC GENITICS!

Did you hear about the guy who was half-Polish and half-Italian?

⇨ *He'd make you an offer you couldn't understand!*

Whaddya get when you cross a Chinese with a Puerto Rican?

⇨ *A car thief who can't drive!*

What about the restaurant that's half-Japanese and half-Jewish?

⇨ *It's called "So-Su-Mi!"*

How about the restaurant that's half-Jewish and half-Mexican?

⇨ *It's called "La Casa Haddassah!"*

How about the restaurant that's half-Mexican and half-Black?

⇨ *It's called "Nacho' Mama!"*

MORE TO COME...

PATHETIC GENETICS!

Then there's the restaurant that's half-German and half-Chinese!

⇨ *You eat there, and an hour later you're hungry...for power!*

You hear about the guy who was half-Black and half-Japanese?

⇨ *Every December 7th, he'd attack Pearl Bailey!*

And how about the restaurant that's half-Gay and half-Chinese?

⇨ *The soup du jour is "Cream of Sum Yung Guy."*

Whaddya get when you cross a Puerto Rican with a Jew?

⇨ *A janitor who thinks he owns the building!*

What do you call Black parachutists in the South?

⇨ *Skeet!*

MORE TO COME...

POLISH YOUR POLISH!
(OR IS IT "POLISH YOUR POLISH?")

Why did God spell Polish and polish the same?

⇨ *Cause he didn't know shit from shinola!*

* * *

A Polish pilot radios to the control tower, telling them he is lost. They say, "We need to know your height and location." He says, "I'm 5' 11" and I'm in the cockpit!"

* * *

A Polish fellow calls the fire department. He says, "You gotta get here in a hurry, my house is on fire!" The fire chief says, "How do we get there?" The fellow replies, "Whatsa matter, don't you have those big, red trucks anymore?"

* * *

A fleet commander during World War II sends out six pilots to drop leaflets over Nazi Germany. Five of them return a few hours later, but the Polack is missing in action. Finally, he returns almost a week later. The commander barks at him, "Wjolenski, how long does it take for you to drop a batch of leaflets over Germany?" He says, "Drop 'em! Shit! I was stickin' 'em under the doorways!"

MORE TO COME...

TOTEM QUOTEMS!

An Indian walks into a bar with a bucket of shit and a dead cat and orders a whiskey. The bartender gives it to him and watches as he gulps down the whiskey, takes out a gun and fires into the bucket, then takes a bite out of the dead cat! The Indian then orders another drink, and proceeds to do the same thing; he gulps down the whiskey, fires his gun into the bucket and takes a bite out of the cat. After several more rounds of this bizarre behavior, the bartender finally says, "Hey, man, I don't mean to pry, but can I ask you why you're doing all that?"

The Indian replies, "Sure, I was just trying to be like white man! I drink 'em whiskey, shoot 'em the shit and eat 'em pussy!"

* * *

Whaddya call a queer Indian?

⇨ *A brave sucker!*

Why was the Chief's daughter called "99 cents?"

⇨ *'Cause she was always under a buck!*

MORE TO COME...

COLOR-COORDINATION!

Whaddya call a white guy between two blacks?

⇨ *In trouble!*

Whaddya call a white guy between five blacks?

⇨ *Coach!*

Whaddya call a white guy between ten blacks?

⇨ *Quarterback!*

Whaddya call a white guy between two thousand blacks?

⇨ *Warden!*

Whaddya call a white guy between 100,000 blacks?

⇨ *Postal Inspector!*

Whaddya call a white guy between 2 million blacks?

⇨ *South African!*

MORE TO COME...

BIASED VIEWS!

How do you recognize a WASP widow?

⇨ *She's the one wearing a black tennis outfit!*

How do you recognize a gay Jewish weightlifter?

⇨ *He's the one pumping Myron!*

How can you tell an Italian cesspool?

⇨ *It's the one with the diving board!*

How do you recognize a Polish rape suspect?

⇨ *He steps out of the police line-up and says, "That's the girl!"*

How can you tell a Polish hijacker?

⇨ *He demands $2.00 and 100,000 parachutes!*

MORE TO COME...

BIASED VIEWS!

How can you tell if you've won the Polish lottery?

⇨ *You win $1 a year for 50,000 years!*

How can you tell an Italian airplane?

⇨ *It's the one with outdoor toilets!*

How can you spot a sexually excited WASP?

⇨ *By his stiff upper lip!*

How can you tell a Polish firing squad?

⇨ *They stand in a circle!*

How can you spot an Italian with class?

⇨ *All the words in his tattoo are spelled correctly!*

MORE TO COME...

HYSTERY OF THE WORLD!

What big party was held in the year 13 A.D.?
⇨ *Jesus' Bar-Mitzvah!*

What happened when Israel attacked Lebanon?
⇨ *The Italians surrendered!*

Why did only 600 Mexicans attack the Alamo?
⇨ *They only had two cars!*

What happened in the year 1550?
⇨ *A Polack invented the toilet seat!*

What happened in the year 1660?
⇨ *An Englishman cut a hole in it!*

MORE TO COME...

HYSTERY OF THE WORLD!

How do we know Lincoln was Jewish?

⇨ *He was shot in the temple!*

Why are Jewish children obnoxious?

⇨ *Heredity!*

What was the weather on Pearl Harbor Day?

⇨ *There was a nip in the air!*

Why did the Jews win the war in six days?

⇨ *Because the tanks were rented!*

When is Polish Culture Day?

⇨ *February 31st!*

MORE TO COME...

CONSUMERS BEWARE!

Have you heard about the new Jewish tires?

⇨ *Firesteins; they not only stop on a dime, but they pick it up, too!*

Have you heard about the new Polish parachute?

⇨ *It opens upon impact!*

Have you heard about the new German microwave?

⇨ *It seats twelve!*

Have you heard about the new Jewish porno movie?

⇨ *It has ten minutes of sex; fifty minutes of guilt!*

Have you heard about the new Polish bank?

⇨ *Give them a toaster, they give you $10,000!*

MORE TO COME...

CONSUMERS BEWARE!

Have you heard about the new Italian mouthwash?

⇨ *It's garlic-flavored!*

Have you heard about the new Polish feminine deodorant spray?

⇨ *It's tuna-flavored!*

Have you heard about the new Irish ladder?

⇨ *The top rung says, "Stop here!"*

Have you heard about the new Polish puzzle?

⇨ *It's one piece!*

Have you heard about the new Italian submarine?

⇨ *It has screen doors!*

MORE TO COME...

CONSUMERS BEWARE!

Have you heard about the new Black clothes dryer?

⇨ *The fire escape!*

Have you heard about the new Polish briefcase?

⇨ *It holds thirty-six pairs of underwear!*

Have you heard about the new Jewish cow?

⇨ *It says, "Nuuuuu!"*

Have you heard about the new Polish sponge?

⇨ *It's waterproof!*

Have you heard about the Polish bumper cars?

⇨ *There's one car!*

MORE TO COME...

RACIAL FEATURES!

Let's say you want a brain transplant. What's the most expensive kind?

⇨ *The Polish model, it's hardly been used!*

Now, you want a penis transplant! A black twelve incher costs $2,500.00! How much does a white one cost?

⇨ *That size doesn't come in white!*

Why do Jewish women have crow's feet around their eyes?

⇨ *From saying, "Suck what?" (and squinting.)*

Why do Jews have short necks?

⇨ *I dunno! (and shrug.)*

Why do Italians have short necks?

⇨ *From saying, "I don't remember," to Grand Juries! (and shrug.)*

More to come...

RACIAL FEATURES!

What does a JAP do to keep her hands soft?

⇨ *Nothing!*

Why do Blacks' rear ends stick out and up?

⇨ *Cause when God asked the first Black man what he wanted, he said, "To get my ass high!"*

Why do Polish women with large vaginas use Crest?

⇨ *Because they read that "It helps to reduce cavities!"*

Why don't Arabs get hemmorhoids?

⇨ *Because they're perfect assholes!*

Why do Italians have pock marked faces?

⇨ *From learning to eat with forks and knives!*

MORE TO COME...

RACIAL FEATURES!

How does God make Puerto Ricans?

⇨ *By sandblasting blacks!*

How do you brainwash an Italian?

⇨ *Give him an enema!*

Why did God give Blacks rhythm?

⇨ *'Cause he fucked up their hair!*

What happens when a Jew with a hard-on walks into a wall?

⇨ *He breaks his nose!*

Why are Italian women so strong?

⇨ *From raising dumbbells!*

MORE TO COME...

LIGHT AND LIVELY JUDAICA!

How does a Jewish woman get her teeth like pearls?

⇨ *She goes to Pearl's dentist!*

How does a JAP commit suicide?

⇨ *She jumps off her clothes!*

How do you make Manischevitz wine?

⇨ *Squeeze his balls!*

How does a JAP lose five pounds?

⇨ *She takes off her make-up!*

How does a Jewish hooker get her fur?

⇨ *Hole Sale!*

MORE TO COME...

RACIAL ROUND-UP!

Why was Alex Haley depressed?

⇨ *He found out he was adopted!*

Did you hear about the Polish kamikaze pilot?

⇨ *He returned successfully from twenty-three missions!*

What does a Norwegian hooker do?

⇨ *Anything for a Finn!*

How does a Polish embezzler operate?

⇨ *He steals the accounts payable!*

Why do Italians make good firemen?

⇨ *They slide down the pole faster!*

MORE TO COME...

RACIAL ROUND-UP!

Did you hear about the Jewish hijacker?

⇨ *He demanded $10 million in pledges!*

What's the largest Jamaican business firm in the country?

⇨ *U.S. Steal!*

Didya hear about the Polish surgeon?

⇨ *He does appendix transplants!*

What are the rules in a Greek wrestling match?

⇨ *"No holes barred!"*

Why was the Japanese hooker starving?

⇨ *Nobody had a yen for her!*

MORE TO COME...

RACIAL ROUND-UP!

How does a JAP charge her vibrator?

⇨ *On American Express!*

How does a Puerto Rican get into a legititmate business?

⇨ *Through the skylight!*

How do you sink an Italian submarine?

⇨ *Put it in the water!*

How do you scare a Black?

⇨ *Give the jig-a-boo!*

How do you circumcise a Black?

⇨ *With a jig-saw!*

MORE TO COME...

RACIAL ROUND-UP!

How do you tickle a JAP?

⇨ *Gucci, Gucci, goo!*

How do you separate the men from the boys in the Greek navy?

⇨ *With a crowbar!*

How can you tell a Polish astronomer?

⇨ *He doesn't work nights!*

How did the Polish couple freeze to death at the Drive-In?

⇨ *They went to see 'Closed For The Winter'!*

How do you make an Irishman laugh on Monday?

⇨ *Tell him a joke on Friday!*

MORE TO COME...

RACIAL ROUND-UP!

How many Ethiopians can you fit into a phone booth?

⇨ *All of them!*

Why don't Puerto Ricans have checking accounts?

⇨ *It's too hard to sign your name with spray paint!*

How do you say 'Fuck you' in Yiddish?

⇨ *"Trust me!"*

How does a Black propose marriage?

⇨ *"You're gonna have a wha'?"*

What does U.J.A. also stand for?

⇨ *Unindicted Jewish Arbitrageurs!*

MORE TO COME...

RACIAL ROUND-UP!

Is it true that all Japanese have cataracts?

⇨ *No, many of them have Rincolns and Chevrorets!*

What are the seven Irish holidays that call for heavy drinking?

⇨ *Monday, Tuesday, Wednesday, etc...*

Can a Chinese couple have a white baby?

⇨ *Yes, Occidents will happen!*

Do most Polish couples have mutual climax?

⇨ *No, many of them have All-State and Prudential!*

How can you tell the WASPs at a Chinese Restaurant?

⇨ *They're the ones not sharing the food!*

MORE TO COME...

RACIAL ROUND-UP!

How do you starve a black man?

⇨ *Hide his food stamps under his work boots!*

What does a WASP say to his wife after love-making?

⇨ *"I'm sorry; it'll never happen again!"*

What does an Indian say to a mermaid before love-making?

⇨ *"How?"*

What does a black man say as he passes a zebra?

⇨ *"Now you see me, now you don't; now you see me..."*

What is the secret of the world's greatest Polish comedian?

⇨ *Uh...uh...uh...ttttiming!*

MORE TO COME...

RACIAL ROUND-UP!

Did you hear about the Polish abortion clinic?

⇨ *There's a ten month waiting list!*

What's the dirtiest four-letter word in Harlem?

⇨ *Work!*

Why does New York have Blacks and California have earthquakes?

⇨ *California had first choice!*

Why do Arabs have oil and Polacks have sausages?

⇨ *The Polacks had first choice!*

Why did God invent the orgasm?

⇨ *So Puerto Ricans would know when to stop screwing!*

More to come...

RACIAL ROUND-UP!

What's an Irish seven-course meal?

⇨ *A baked potato and a six-pack!*

Why did God invent Golf?

⇨ *He wanted to give white folks a chance to dress up like Black folks!*

Why did God create WASPs?

⇨ *Somebody had to pay retail!*

Why did the Mexicans fight so hard for the Alamo?

⇨ *They needed four clean walls to write on!*

How can you tell if a camera's Japanese?

⇨ *If it goes 'crick!'*

MORE TO COME...

WHAT'S DE-MEANING?

DEFINE THE FOLLOWING:

JAP's dream house:
> Twelve rooms in Scarsdale with no kitchen or bedroom!

Queer Jew:
> Someone who likes women more than money!

Diaphragm:
> A trampoline for schmucks!

Election:
> What a Chinese blide-gloom gets!

Wiener:
> The first to finish in a Mexican race!

Black insomniac:
> The fellow who keeps waking up every few days!

JAP's ideal sex:
> Simultaneous headaches!

MORE TO COME...

WHAT'S DE-MEANING?

DEFINE THE FOLLOWING:

Piece de resistance:
> A French virgin!

Jewish nympho:
> A girl who will have sex right after the beauty parlor!

Fuck off:
> The tiebreaker in an Italian beauty contest!

Minimum:
> A small British mom!

Bigamist:
> A fog over Rome!

Operetta:
> An Italian girl who works for the phone company!

Fart:
> A Greek mating call!

MORE TO COME...

WHAT'S DE MEANING?

DEFINE THE FOLLOWING:

Chutzpah:
> A young man who kills both his parents and then pleads for leniency because he's an orphan!

Jewish dilemma:
> A half-priced sale on bacon!

Mass confusion:
> Father's Day in Harlem!

J.A.P.'s natural childbirth:
> Absolutely no make-up!

Nice Greek boy:
> One who will date a girl a few times before he propositions...her brother!

Fellatio:
> The French connection!

Prune foo yung:
> Chinese food **to go!**

MORE TO COME...

WHAT'S DE MEANING?

DEFINE THE FOLLOWING:

Bigotry:

An Italian Redwood!

WASP:

Someone who steps out of the shower to pee!

French Asthma:

You can only catch your breath in snatches!

Wrench:

A Jewish resort with horses!

Redneck:

Someone who will screw a Black girl but won't go to school with her!

Reneg:

The shift change at Burger King!

Optimist:

An Ethiopian in a dinner jacket!

MORE TO COME...

CROSS-UPS!

Whaddya get when you cross a Black with a WASP?

⇨ *An abortion!*

Whaddya get when you cross a Black and a Mexican?

⇨ *A car thief too lazy to steal!*

How about when you cross a Mexican and an Iranian?

⇨ *Oil of Ole!*

How 'bout when you cross a Black and a Jewish accountant?

⇨ *A guy who says, "Slip me 5...percent!"*

Whaddya get when you cross a one-legged Polack and a Mongoloid?

⇨ *A Polaroid one-step!*

MORE TO COME...

CROSS-UPS!

WHADDYA GET WHEN YOU CROSS THE FOLLOWING:

A Black and a Russian?

⇨ *Hammer and Sickle-Cell Anemia!*

A Black and a Southern Woman?

⇨ *A lynching!*

A Puerto Rican and a Gorilla?

⇨ *Black people!*

Bo Derek and Diana Ross?

⇨ *The 10 of Spades!*

A monkey and a Black?

⇨ *Don't be stupid! A monkey wouldn't fuck a
Black person!*

MORE TO COME...

FALSE OCCUPANCY!

SANTA CLAUS	A SMART POLACK
A DUMB POLACK	THE EASTER BUNNY

WHICH ONE DOESN'T BELONG IN THE ROOM ABOVE?

⇨ *The Dumb Polack! There's no such thing as the other three!*

MORE TO COME...

PRE-LAY RACES!

IRISH foreplay:
⇨ "Brace yourself, Maggie!"

BLACK foreplay:
⇨ "Scream and I'll kill you!"

JEWISH foreplay:
⇨ Two hours of pleading and begging!

ITALIAN foreplay:
⇨ "Eh, c'mere, bitch!"

W.A.S.P. foreplay:
⇨ Drying the dishes together!

AUSTRALIAN foreplay:
⇨ Baaaaa! Baaaaa!

POLISH foreplay:
⇨ "Are you awake?"

MORE TO COME...

RACY PICTURES!

WHAT IS THIS?

IN

←—————————————

OUT

—————————————→

(REPEAT AS NECESSARY)

ANSWER: A POLISH SEX MANUAL!

MORE TO COME...

THE JAP RAP!

Why won't a barracuda attack a JAP?
> ⇨ *Professional courtesy!*

Does a JAP consider sex: work or pleasure?
> ⇨ *Pleasure, of course! Otherwise, she'd hire a schvartze to do it!*

What does a JAP do to her asshole every morning?
> ⇨ *She sends him to work!*

Why do JAPs like wonton soup?
> ⇨ *Because spelled backwards, it "NOT NOW!"*

Why do JAPs like circumcised men?
> ⇨ *They like anything that's twenty percent off!*

MORE TO COME...

THE POLACK RAP

How do you confuse a Polish laborer?
> *Throw down three shovels and tell him to take his pick!*

Did you hear about the Polack who bought a toilet brush?
> *Two weeks later, he was back to using toilet paper!*

Did you hear about the Polack who went to Vegas?
> *He lost all his money in the parking meters!*

Why are there so many epileptics in the Polish army?
> *Because they figure, this way, the enemy won't be able to tell who's wounded!*

What's black and crispy and hangs from the chandelier?
> *A Polish electrician!*

MORE TO COME...

DID YOU HEAR ABOUT THE POLACK THAT...

Did you hear about the Polish loan shark?

⇨ *He loaned out money all over town and then skipped!*

Did you hear the latest Polish knock-knock joke?

⇨ *You start!*

Did you hear about the Polish guy who's wife told him she wanted foreplay?

⇨ *He went out and got three more guys!*

Did you hear how the Polish guy died in a helicopter?

⇨ *He got cold and shut off the fan!*

MORE TO COME...

TACTLESS FACTS!

A Polish girl will never marry a bisexual!
⇨ *Sex twice a year is not enough!*

All JAPs love to play Ms. Pac-man!
⇨ *Sure! You can get eaten three times for a quarter!*

Italian garbagemen are well-paid!
⇨ *$300 per week and all they can eat!*

Frenchmen have trouble getting their wives pregnant!
⇨ *They keep muffing it!*

Batman is Polish!
⇨ *Who else would wear their jockey shorts over their leotard!*

MORE TO COME...

TACTLESS FACTS!

The last Russian beauty queen's measurements were 36"-26"-36"!

⇨ *And her other leg was the same size!*

Polacks have special car insurance!

⇨ *It's called, "My Fault!"*

An Italian sees his priest three times in his life!

⇨ *When he's born, when he's married and when he's executed!*

You should never take shit from a Polack!

⇨ *It may be his lunch!*

The average age of the Irish soldier is 45!

⇨ *Yes, they get them right out of high school!*

MORE TO COME...

TACTLESS FACTS!

All JAPs are on a diet trying to get back to their original weight!
　⇨ *Yes, 7 lbs., 8 oz.!*

Blacks will not accept blowjobs!
　⇨ *They don't want to jeopardize their unemployment benefits!*

Chinese hookers make the most money!
　⇨ *Their customers come back horny an hour later!*

Suntan lotion will not work for Polacks!
　⇨ *No matter how much they drink!*

JAPs know a lot about Fucking and Sucking!
　⇨ *Sure, it's two cities in China!*

MORE TO COME...

TACTLESS FACTS!

JAPs cannot wear chastity belts!
> ⇨*Jewish men love to eat locks! (lox)*

Blacks wear white gloves while eating Tootsie Rolls!
> ⇨*Sure, so they don't bite off the tips of their fingers!*

All Black males' penises are two inches!
> ⇨*From the ground!*

A JAP is asked many times to get married in her life!
> ⇨*By her parents!*

Polacks make the best secret agents!
> ⇨*Yes, even if they're tortured, they still can't remember their mission!*

MORE TO COME...

TACTLESS FACTS!

There is a Jewish Santa!
⇨ *He comes down the chimney and sells toys cheap!*

Polacks do not make good parachutists!
⇨ *They miss the earth!*

Italian girls usually wear wool skirts!
⇨ *And it's easy to pull the wool over their eyes!*

All male Jewish babies are the same size!
⇨ *They're all circum-sized!*

There are no good seats at Warsaw Stadium!
⇨ *You're always sitting behind a Pole!*

MORE TO COME...

TACTLESS FACTS!

A Jewish man will not report his credit cards stolen!
> ⇨ *He figures the thief will spend less than his wife!*

All helicopters are Italian!
> ⇨ *They go:*
> *wop...wop...wop...guinea...guinea...guinea...*

There are usually four major participants at a Puerto Rican wedding!
> ⇨ *The bride, the groom and the two kids!*

Orthodox rabbis are the worst drivers!
> ⇨ *They're always cutting someone off!*

Polish women use glass diaphragms!
> ⇨ *They want a "womb with a view!"*

MORE TO COME...

TACTLESS FACTS!

A Polack will not buy an A.M. radio!
  ⇨ *What if he wants to listen in the P.M.?*

It's O.K. to tell a Polack a Polish joke!
  ⇨ *Just tell it slowly!*

You can always tell a Jewish baby at the nursery!
  ⇨ *He's the one with the heartburn!*

Puerto Ricans shoot at cans with B.B. guns!
  ⇨ *Yeah, Mexi-cans, Afri-cans,...*

Blacks keep chickens in the backyard!
  ⇨ *To teach their children how to walk!*

MORE TO COME...

TACTLESS QUESTIONS!

What does a Polish woman get that's long and hard on her wedding night?

⇨ *A new last name!*

Whaddya call four black guys in a new Cadillac?

⇨ *Grand Theft Auto!*

Whaddya get when you cross a JAP with a computer?

⇨ *A system that won't go down!*

What's two miles long and has an I.Q. of 50?

⇨ *The St. Patrick's Day Parade!*

Why do Polish kids make good astronauts?

⇨ *Because they take up space in school!*

MORE TO COME...

NAME IT DEFAME IT !

Whaddya call a Greek tampon?

⇒ *Ab-Zorba!*

How about Greek lipstick?

⇒ *Preparation-H!*

Whaddya call a WASP toy store?

⇒ *'Goys-R-Us'!*

How about a toy store in Harlem?

⇒ *'We-Be-Toys'!*

What does a Black kid get for Christmas?

⇒ *Your bike!*

MORE TO COME...

NAME IT, DEFAME IT!

WHADDYA CALL:

A gay Mexican?

⇨ *A senor-eater!*

A gay guy from Tokyo?

⇨ *A Japansie!*

A Black on a horse?

⇨ *Le-Roy Rogers!*

A Polack chasing a garbage truck?

⇨ *The Galloping Gourmet!*

Oral sex in London?

⇨ *English muffin!*

MORE TO COME...

NAME IT, DEFAME IT!

WHADDYA CALL:

A Mexican gigolo?
⇨ *Juan-for-the-money!*

A pelvic exam in Japan?
⇨ *Nooki-Looki!*

Catholics who use rhythm method of birth control?
⇨ *Mom and Dad!*

Kraft's factory in Israel?
⇨ *Cheeses of Nazareth!*

An Ethiopian in Colombia?
⇨ *A stick in the mud!*

MORE TO COME...

NAME IT DEFAME IT!

WHADDYA CALL:

Whaddya call twelve black men in a courtroom?
⇨ *A hung jury!*

Whaddya call an uncircumsized Jewish baby?
⇨ *A Girl!*

Whaddya call a Puerto Rican hitchhiker?
⇨ *Stranded!*

Whaddya call a beautiful girl in Poland?
⇨ *A Tourist!*

MORE TO COME...

NAME IT, DEFAME IT!

WHADDYA CALL:

A French soap opera that takes place in the ladies' room?

⇨ *Bidets of our Lives!*

A 75-pound Ethiopian?

⇨ *Fatso!*

A Chinese voyeur?

⇨ *Peking Tom!*

French self-defense?

⇨ *Tung-Fu!*

A police raid in Russia?

⇨ *Drag Nyet!*

MORE TO COME...

NAME IT, DEFAME IT!

WHADDYA CALL:

A Polack with a degree?

⇨ *Liar!*

A disco in Israel?

⇨ *The Let My People Go-Go!*

A field of Blacks buried in the dirt up to their eyebrows?

⇨ *Afro-turf!*

One thousand JAPs heading towards Bloomingdale's?

⇨ *Yidlock!*

The sawdust on the floor of an Irish bar?

⇨ *Last night's furniture!*

MORE TO COME...

NAME IT, DEFAME IT!

WHADDYA CALL:

A JAPs nipple?

⇨ *The tip of the iceberg!*

An Italian diaphragm?

⇨ *A wopstopper!*

A ruptured Chinaman?

⇨ *Won Hung Lo!*

A JAPs waterbed?

⇨ *Lake Placid or the Dead Sea!*

An Oriental grocery clerk?

⇨ *Chinese checker!*

MORE TO COME...

NAME IT, DEFAME IT!

WHADDYA CALL:

A Russian condom?

⇨ *Red Riding Hood!*

A safe in Warsaw?

⇨ *A Pole vault!*

A German tampon?

⇨ *Twatsticker!*

Two Black motorcycle cops?

⇨ *Chocolate Chips!*

A Black with no arms and legs?

⇨ *Dot!*

MORE TO COME...

NAME IT, DEFAME IT!

WHADDYA CALL:

A Puerto Rican's zipper?

⇨ *Spanish fly!*

A Jew who really knows how to control a wife?

⇨ *Bachelor!*

A Catholic weekend?

⇨ *Payday, Playday, Prayday!*

A surrogate parent in Stockholm?

⇨ *An artificial Swedener!*

An Italian slum?

⇨ *A spaghetto!*

MORE TO COME...

NAME IT, DEFAME IT!

WHADDYA CALL:

American Indian swing parties?

⇨*Passing the Buck!*

Israelis who work for Sun-Kist?

⇨*Orange Jews!*

A Norwegian car?

⇨*A Fjord!*

A gay Arab comedian?

⇨*Tongue-in-shiek!*

An Italian suppository?

⇨*Innuendo!*

MORE TO COME...

NAME IT, DEFAME IT!

WHADDYA CALL:

The 'seven year itch' in Poland?

⇨ *Crabs!*

The chief Jew in Alaska?

⇨ *Eskimoses!*

A Black test-tube baby?

⇨ *A Janitor in a Drum!*

A Puerto Rican baby doctor?

⇨ *Dr. Spic!*

A lightning attack by the Israelis?

⇨ *A Blintzkrieg!*

MORE TO COME...

NAME IT, DEFAME IT!

WHADDYA CALL:

A Negro whore with braces?

⇨ *A Black and Decker pecker wrecker!*

A virgin Squaw?

⇨ *A wouldn't Indian!*

An Egyptian girl not on the pill?

⇨ *A Mummy!*

A Black skindiver?

⇨ *Jacques Custodian!*

An Indian with three balls?

⇨ *A buck and a half!*

MORE TO COME...

NAME IT, DEFAME IT!

WHADDYA CALL:

The Negro social register?

⇨ *The Blacklist!*

An Indian jock-strap?

⇨ *Totem Pole!*

A funny Canadian policeman?

⇨ *Mountie Python!*

A football game between the Italians and the Polacks?

⇨ *The Toilet Bowl!*

A Mexican Negro?

⇨ *A wetblack!*

MORE TO COME...

NAME IT, DEFAME IT!

WHADDYA CALL:

A sexy Italian woman?

⇨ *A 'pizza' ass!*

A guy who's half Polish and half Chinese?

⇨ *Sum Dum Fuk!*

A Black woman in the Army?

⇨ *A WAC-coon!*

A Black neckwear salesman?

⇨ *A tie-coon!*

A fag in Ireland?

⇨ *Home O' Sexual!*

MORE TO COME...

NAME IT, DEFAME IT!

WHADDYA CALL:

An Oriental on 'ludes?
⇨ *Mellow Yellow!*

A Jewish private detective agency?
⇨ *Renta Yenta!*

A Black 'Preparation-H' salesman?
⇨ *An 'ass-cream' coon!*

An Israeli spy plane?
⇨ *A Jew-2!*

Richard Pryor and Michael Jackson's charity?
⇨ *The Ignited Negro College Fund!*

MORE TO COME...

NAME IT, DEFAME IT!

WHADDYA CALL:

An Italian folk-dance?

⇨ *A wop hop!*

A Polish folk-dance?

⇨ *A goof-ball!*

A Polack in a tree?

⇨ *Branch Manager!*

A collection of German fairy tales?

⇨ *Mother Goose-step!*